Praise for *Holy Friendships*

"Every Christian called to leadership should read this book. In *Holy Friendships*, the Rev. Dr. Victoria Atkinson White invites our attention to an underexplored aspect of the walk of faith: namely, that it's more than relationship with God and relationship with a community. The intimate, tender, and sacred connections with Dear Ones who walk alongside us are vital for discipleship and leadership discernment. Her work convicted me as a leader walking too many days alone. Her words also joyfully prompted me to call close friends, express the value of our relationship, and spend time 'holding their basket' when necessary."

—**Rev. Dr. Starsky Wilson**, president and CEO, Children's Defense Fund and CDF Action Council, and board chair for the National Committee for Responsive Philanthropy and the Forum for Theological Exploration

"Victoria's heart shines through in *Holy Friendships*—her genuine love for pastors and leaders and her desire for their flourishing. In an age when relationships have become increasingly diluted and dispersed in many ways, she shines a light on a different possibility of friendship rooted in pragmatic simplicity. Hence, her definition, 'Holy friendships are mutual and sacred relationships deeply formed in God's love,' shows us how essential it is for holy friendships to be intentionally cultivated and engaged by individuals. She gives us tools for how to think about them. So, I'm grateful for the meaningful work she has done in these conversations and how it opens space for us to consider the serious importance of friendships, not only for our flourishment but for our very survival."

—**Mihee Kim-Kort**, pastor and author of *Outside the Lines:*
How Embracing Queerness Will Transform Your Faith

"The cost of critique is a better alternative than the status quo, and Victoria Atkinson White offers precisely that wisdom in this moving and inspiring book. Burnout culture among faith leaders cannot be solved by the latest productivity hack or a weeklong retreat from reality. Our path forward must begin with our most authentic connections—to self, community, and God. White offers a lifeline for all of us struggling to find balance in an increasingly off-kilter world, and she does so with grace and humor. The holy friendships she features, including several of her own, will leave you feeling inspired to go deeper with some of your own friends and see those relationships as a core part of your leadership life, not something to tend to once your 'real' work is done."

—**Rabbi Elan Babchuck**, founder of Glean Network and executive vice president, National Jewish Center for Learning and Leadership

"Writing with passionate advocacy, Victoria Atkinson White charts a pathway that will guide pastoral leaders toward flourishing in their vocations. Without holy friendships that call for accountability, provide support, and validate identity, none of us could continue faithfully in our callings. Life is too difficult to do it alone, White wisely perceives. She names the role that holy friends can play not only in the rough patches but in making all of life more satisfying. It is an ancient practice given new form through White's careful research and personal experience. Reading her winsome book helped me name my holy friends and seek to be a better one."

—**Rev. Dr. Molly T. Marshall**, president,
United Theological Seminary of the Twin Cities

"In the face of isolating forces such as the Covid-19 pandemic and fraying of our social fabric, our need for belonging endures. With a personal touch and an accessible style, White reminds us that God made us for community, and invites us to seek and sustain holy friendships. Far from being a waste of precious time, such relationships are essential for personal health, vocational fulfillment, and communal flourishing."

—**Edgardo Colón-Emeric**, dean, Duke Divinity School,
and author of *The People Called Metodista: Renewing
Doctrine, Worship, and Mission from the Margins*

"This is a deeply wise and hopeful text. While Victoria Atkinson White is clear-eyed and realistic about the challenges that pastoral leaders especially face in cultivating and maintaining holy friendships, her book abounds with winsome and sage advice about how to do so and, even more valuably, embodied narratives about why these friendships are worth the investiture of intentionality. In the work of vulnerable relationality that is needed now more than ever, White's book is both guide and gift."

—**Robert Saler**, assistant professor of theology and
culture, and director of the Lilly Endowment Clergy
Renewal Programs, Christian Theological Seminary

"My life has been sustained by deep friendships that have helped and supported me in ways I can't fully express. Victoria Atkinson White has captured my experience in words and helped me appreciate the rich gift of holy friendship. If you need holy friends, have them already, or simply want to learn what difference they might make in your life, I highly recommend *Holy Friendships*."

—**Brian D. McLaren**, author of *Do I Stay Christian? A Guide for the Doubters, the Disappointed, and the Disillusioned*

"Victoria White's debut book is a sensation, and easily the most timely, most urgently needed, most soul-searching book I've read in years. Every page is laced with honesty and compassion, bolstered by research and enough biblical discussion to land *Holy Friendships* on the must-read list for seminarians, future preachers, and congregational leaders for years to come. But it's White's charm as a storyteller that sneaks up on you. It kept me reading until I finally realized what was happening. White isn't just describing holy friendship in these pages—she's extending it. Thanks be to God."

—**Kenda Creasy Dean**, Mary D. Synnott Professor of Youth, Church, and Culture, Princeton Theological Seminary, and author of *Innovating for Love: Joining God's Expedition through Christian Social Innovation* and *Almost Christian: What the Faith of Our Teenagers Is Telling the American Church*

"Ministers are healthiest when they work in sync with the rhythmic pulse of the divine life of love. In this insightful book, Victoria Atkinson White describes the sustaining power of holy friendships that gives pastors and other leaders hope and help in a calling that requires so much personal vulnerability. The giving and receiving of holy friendships are the secret of lifelong well-being in ministry."

—**Rev. Dr. George A. Mason**, president of Faith Commons and author of *Preparing the Pastors We Need: Reclaiming the Congregation's Role in Training Clergy*

"What if a joyful meal, a quiet walk, a text thread, or a difficult conversation can all be sources of grace and hope in a divided world? In this delightful book, Victoria White invites us to appreciate again the many ways that holy friendships can transform us and make us new. Through story and wit, wise insight and careful listening, this book is an ideal companion for those of us called into the often-lonely roads of leadership, teaching us that it does not have to be lonely. Friendship is not just essential. Friendship is a sacred practice and can even become a vivid reflection of God's own love."

—**Eric D. Barreto**, Weyerhaeuser Associate Professor of New Testament, Princeton Theological Seminary

"Every reader who opens this book will immediately recognize the holy friendships in their lives, friendships that provide sustenance for the punishing work of leadership. And every leader who opens this book will immediately recognize the places in their own lives where the lack of holy friendships has left arid, wounded, and broken spaces that are so very difficult to heal. As the institutions we serve shift, this book is set to become a critically important addition to the fundamental training faith leaders need to lead well, survive that work, and thrive. Learning to identify, gather, and nurture holy friendships is, of course, an essential key to leadership with lasting impact, but when you read Dr. White's words, you will know that they are also guideposts on the journey to a healed and whole life."

—**Rev. Dr. Amy K. Butler**, founder and president, Invested Faith, and former senior minister, the Riverside Church in the city of New York

"Friendship—holy friendship—is an indispensable leadership practice. With this good news, Victoria Atkinson White invites us to a transformed experience of leadership marked by joy, companionship, and the freedom that comes from a deep sense of our belovedness before God and dear friends. Leaders seeking a flourishing way of life that can nourish them and their communities should read this book as a vital step toward receiving the life-sustaining gifts of holy friendships."

—**Aaron Kuecker**, interim president and professor of New Testament, Trinity Christian College

"Christian leadership is too difficult to be done solo. Victoria White gives us a wonderful testimony to the joy (and necessity) of friendship. She shows how friendship is at the core of the practice of Christian faith and how friendship with Christ enables us to cultivate and sustain friendship with people who support us in our sometimes demanding vocations."

—**Will Willimon**, professor of the practice of Christian ministry, Duke Divinity School; retired United Methodist bishop; and author of *Accidental Preacher: A Memoir*

"Victoria White graciously and brilliantly invites us to cultivate our own holy friendships and encourages us to evaluate these relationships in different seasons of our life. We are drawn in by her personal stories of evolving holy friendships and a captivating collection of diverse voices sharing their own stories and reflections. *Holy Friendships* is a beautiful testament to the power of sacred connection, God's desire for us to have deep belonging with those we are in community with, and what it means to be loved, seen, and known beyond the surface. This book serves as a holy nudge to pastors and faith leaders that there is, in fact, life beyond work and that having deeply rooted friendships matters if we are to navigate this crazy world as healthy and whole people of God."

—**Rev. Dr. Aqueelah Ligonde**, vice president of coaching and training, Ministry Incubators, and director of coaching, Ministry Architects

"Victoria Atkinson White hit the nail on the head. Ministry can be a lonely vocation. The artful way in which she tells stories of holy friendships is both a gift and a challenge to anyone who wants to thrive in this calling."

—**Rev. Prince Raney Rivers, PhD**, senior pastor, Union Baptist Church, Durham, North Carolina; consulting faculty member, Duke Divinity School; and author of *John, 1–3 John* (Preaching the Word)

"This is a healing and insightful book about friendships that enhances our ability to thrive as we share our gifts of ministry. We are encouraged, inspired, convinced, and directed toward the nurturing of relationships as holy spaces. This is a treasure for a dimension of spiritual formation needed in our time."

—**Elizabeth Conde-Frazier**, former pastor, professor of practical theology, and academic dean; director, Association for Hispanic Theological Education; and author of *Atando Cabos: Latinx Contributions to Theological Education*

"*Holy Friendships* offers a powerful gift to ministers today. Not only does Victoria Atkinson White establish a compelling biblical and theological foundation for unique and sacred relationships formed in God's love, but she also offers compelling testimony for how these friendships are essential to the thriving and health of pastoral leaders. This book inspires me to more deeply understand the holy friendships that have helped me thrive and to offer profound gratitude for them, while also challenging me to be still more open to being a holy friend to others."

—**Paul Baxley**, executive coordinator,
Cooperative Baptist Fellowship

"Week after week, season after season, decade after decade, so many pastors (I'm preaching to myself here) pour out energy and interest, kindness and counsel, for their people. Victoria's assertion that we can't keep it up, all that emotional export, without serious damage to our own spirits and considerable risk to the very people for whom we do it, is right on time. Our mega-connectedness is all the more draining. It's no wonder that reports of inappropriate relationships by clergy are on the rise. What if we invested ourselves in healthy relationships, even these holy friendships Victoria describes? Maybe we would find our own joyful response to God's call replenished and restored. What a wonder, what an amazing grace, that would be."

—**Rev. Dr. Katie Hays**, founder and lead
evangelist, Galileo Church, Fort Worth, Texas,
and author of *God Gets Everything God Wants*

Holy Friendships

Holy Friendships

Nurturing Relationships That Sustain Pastors and Leaders

Victoria Atkinson White

Foreword by L. Gregory Jones

Fortress Press
Minneapolis

HOLY FRIENDSHIPS
Nurturing Relationships That Sustain Pastors and Leaders

All Scripture quotations are from the New Revised Standard Version Bible, copyright © 1989 National Council of the Churches of Christ in the United States of America. Used by permission. All rights reserved worldwide.

Cover design: Marti Naughton
Cover illustration: Segmented circles 291174414 © pixxsa | Adobe Stock; watercolor 1366177704 © Praewpailin | iStock Photo

Print ISBN: 978-1-5064-8237-8
eBook ISBN: 978-1-5064-8238-5

To Mark, Ava, and Owen

Contents

Foreword

Victoria Atkinson White's book is a beautiful and eloquent witness to the significance of friendship in well-lived lives and flourishing societies. It is both evocative and practical, helping us see how and why friendship matters so much. And she does so within the context of convictions about, and the priority of, God's love as that which undergirds and enables us to discover and sustain meaningful, holy friendships.

Yet this eminently readable book contains a deeper challenge to us than its beautiful, disarming prose and poignant stories might suggest. It would be a mistake to read this book simply as an enrichment to our daily lives, an optional frosting that can enhance an already good life. To take friendship seriously, to evoke the notion that it is connected to holiness in our relationship with God, is to begin a process of examining deeper assumptions of what it means to be human and what is at stake for any of us, much less all of us, to flourish.

To understand why that is the case, it is important to offer a very brief and oversimplified historical overview. Throughout most of the history of Western cultures, friendship was a central category to describe a well-lived life. Plato and Aristotle both highlighted the significance of friendship in their work, and Aristotle, in particular, made friendship the heart of his *Nicomachean Ethics*. Friendship was an important theme in the work of Augustine and Aquinas as well as countless monastic writers such as Aelred of Rievaulx.

This should not be surprising to Christians since Jesus himself calls his disciples friends in the farewell discourses of John's Gospel. And many Christians are familiar with the theme, inaugurated in the Genesis story of the creation of Adam and Eve and highlighted in the opening pages of Augustine's *Confessions*, that we are created for relationship—with God and with one another. Yet even among Christians, the theme of friendship has largely been absent for several centuries.

Indeed, the eclipse of any serious attention to the ethical significance of friendship is characteristic of modern life across the intellectual disciplines as well as in popular cultures. Why would this be so? A combination of factors, including the fragmentation of Christian witness in the Reformation, the rise of a preoccupation with the individual self and eventual emergence of individualism, and development of modes of ethical reasoning more focused on decisions than on character and virtue, all conspired to push the consideration of friendship to the margins. Most textbooks on ethics in modernity would not even mention friendship as a topic, much less make it central to an ethical life.

Friendship has been marginalized in intellectual discourse about the well-lived life; it has also been trivialized in popular cultures. "Friends" are now a category on Facebook, and many people count thousands of "friends." Popular discourse suggests that we describe as "friends" people whom we have barely met, who might otherwise be described, at best, as acquaintances. Aristotle thought a person would be blessed who could count a handful of people as friends at the end of their lives; we seem to think you can make a handful of friends at a single party.

Further, as Christopher Lasch noted in his important 1979 work *The Culture of Narcissism*, the 20th century was increasingly marked by a narcissism that occluded any attempts to connect people meaningfully to one another—a trend that has continued into the 21st century. Recent studies have shown that, despite the trivialization of friendship, the number of actual close friends people have has decreased significantly over the last two decades.

Fortunately, over the past forty years friendship has begun to make a comeback in intellectual discussions about ethics. This was prompted in many ways by Alasdair MacIntyre's widely influential book *After Virtue* and Stanley Hauerwas's *A Community of Character*, both of which were published in 1981. Both books sought to retrieve an Aristotelian approach to ethics as the most compelling way to address deep moral, social, and political challenges in Western life. Although neither MacIntyre nor Hauerwas particularly emphasized friendship in their work at this point, the reemergence of an Aristotelian approach into intellectual debates brought friendship back into more conversations than had been the case for several centuries.

My interest in friendship as an important theme emerged in this context while I was beginning to develop my own theological vocation. I was a student of Hauerwas in the 1980s, and as we read work by Aristotle, Augustine, and Aquinas, I was struck by the importance of friendship for the moral life. I was also intrigued by its prominence in Jesus's farewell discourses in John. An earlier student of Hauerwas when he was at Notre Dame, Paul Wadell, was writing beautifully about friendship by probing deeply into Aquinas's thought. I wrote my dissertation on the significance of friendship and practices in shaping a Christian vision of wise moral judgment, a revised version of which appeared in 1989 as the book *Transformed Judgment*.

My focus in that work was on the ways Aquinas's understanding of friendship with God transformed Aristotle's approach to friendship. I was intrigued by the fact that Aquinas notes that charity is to be understood as "friendship with God," and that charity for Aquinas is "the form of the virtues." I wanted to explore those connections: how a developing friendship with God would shape character (including my own), and lead to a way of thinking about friendship with others and what it means to befriend others, including "unlikely" others, as I had been befriended by Christ.

The idea of holy friendship that my wife, Susan, and I developed and began teaching and writing about (in essays and as a part of books) emerged out of that focus on friendship with God and the journey toward holiness. Drawing on our study of, and experience with, Wesleyan small groups (historically, the class meetings and bands of Wesley's time), Susan and I focused on the ways friends would help each other in their Christian growth. That is why we developed the formulation that was intentional about what we need to unlearn (the sins we have come to love), learn (the gifts we are afraid to claim), and dream (the dreams we otherwise would never have dreamed). Our focus was on the centrality of friendship to help us on a journey of increasing intimacy in friendship with God, a journey of holiness.

In a complementary way, Victoria White's thoughtful account develops the notion of holy friendship by focusing especially on the importance of friendship. To be sure, her formulation accentuates that these are "mutual and sacred relationships deeply formed in God's love." As she further notes, "holy friends participate in our lives in a triune way. They root us in God's ongoing story by validating our past, holding space for us in our present, and helping us midwife a vision for the future." There is a deep connection to the story of God in her vision of holy friendship.

Yet the power of her account, in my view, is found in the beautiful texture of the human friendships she describes in her stories. People long for the mutuality and sacredness of relationships that she describes and illumines. We can learn from these stories concrete practices to help us cultivate more attentiveness to human relationships that matter.

I would be grateful for this book whenever it was published; its appearance now is particularly timely. The last several years have been exceedingly tough as we have navigated multiple pandemics. In addition to the travails of COVID-19, we have experienced in new ways the complexities of racial injustice, economic disruption, political polarization, and an intensification of mental health crises of loneliness, anxiety, depression, and suicide. We live in a time of what Johann Hari called, in a book that appeared shortly before the pandemic in 2018, *Lost Connections*.

I hope that Victoria White's beautiful description of the significance of friendship, and of holy friendships, will contribute to a rediscovery of deep and broad connections. Nothing less than our own moral formation, and the cultivation of gifts necessary for flourishing, depend on such rediscovery.

L. Gregory Jones
President, Belmont University
September 2022

Preface

In my work as a pastor to pastors, I witness the tremendous load Christian leaders bear to do their work. These brave, bold, and passionate leaders feel a call from God to sacrificially lead their communities to flourish through faith in a God who loves the world with reckless abandon. Often, following that call in a quickly changing world results in exhaustion, anxiety, and apathy that lead to collapse.

As religious institutions increasingly grasp for resources, Christian leaders are especially burnt out, isolated, alone, and left to fend for themselves in a world that cannot comprehend their pain. To make matters more dire, pastors tackle a profession that makes asking for help especially hard, so leaders often do not voice their distress until it's too late. And so we (pastors and Christian leaders) are learning again what we so easily forget: ministry is not sustainable when a leader is alone. God made us to be in community.

In my work, I support and study strategies to sustain Christian institutions and their leaders. Within many Christian institutions, I observe the ready assumption that "sustainability" means financial viability. And while financial viability is one aspect of an institution's sustainability, it is not the most essential factor necessary for nurturing a healthy and robust institutional life. An institution cannot thrive if its leaders are not healthy, so my first question to harried pastors and Christian leaders trying to keep their churches and institutions afloat is always, How do you invest in your own sustainability?

What are you doing to keep yourself healthy—physically, emotionally, spiritually, financially, socially, and intellectually? Tell me: What is your sustainability plan?

It's a simple fact: healthy institutions are led by healthy leaders.

At this point in the conversation, pastoral leaders look at me bewildered, because their recognition of their loneliness and lack of healthy social relationships confronts them in ways they cannot ignore. They realize they have fallen into patterns and practices of isolation that have become so familiar they feel like normal life. Tired and lonely, they've forgotten the hope and possibility that led them to this work in the first place.

"So what are we supposed to do? What does investing in our sustainability look like?" they ask, hoping for an easy answer. And I always start my answer here: cultivating and nurturing holy friendships is critical to human flourishing. Pastors and Christian institutional leaders cannot do the holy work they are called to do without holy friends.

Holy friendships are mutual and sacred relationships deeply formed in God's love. Mutuality comes from acknowledging the feeling of belonging that bonds holy friends together. They share a sense of reciprocity between them. Sacred refers to the "set apart–ness" of holy friendships because they are more intentional, more intimate, and different from ordinary friendships; they are holy, and they are "regarded with or deserving deep respect, awe, reference or adoration."[1] Because holy friendships are deeply formed in God's love, we incarnate God's love to one another. In loving our holy friends, we are also loving God, loving ourselves, and loving our neighbors. We will dive deeper into each of these descriptors in chapter 1.

Furthermore, holy friends participate in our lives in a triune way. They root us in God's ongoing story by validating our past, holding space for us in our present, and helping us midwife a vision for the future. First, whether these friends were alongside us when formative events occurred, they validate our experience and help us discern healthy ways to live in our present and plan for our future. Second, by "holding space," a term borrowed from counseling and other listening-based therapies, holy friends cultivate an unconditional safe space where we are confident we can be vulnerable, our most authentic selves. When holy friends hold space for each other, we create an environment in which we both feel spiritually, mentally, physically, and emotionally safe and accepted for who we are as children of God. Third, holy friends help us midwife a vision for the future because they see us as key contributors in God's ongoing love story with creation. Holy friends push us to dream bigger, aim higher, and trust God more fully than we would on our own.

Thanks to the generosity of my wise colleagues at Leadership Education at Duke Divinity School, the generosity of the Louisville Institute Pastoral Study Project Grant Program, the Guthrie Scholars Program at the Center for Lifelong Learning at Columbia Theological Seminary, and my students and colleagues at the Institute for Youth Ministry at Princeton Theological Seminary, I have interviewed pastors and other Christian leaders and mused on, discussed, and explored the holy friendships that are critical to their sustainability and flourishing. I know holy friends are essential because this truth is evident in the lives of the hundreds of exemplary pastors and Christian leaders who shared with me their stories about these key relationships that make their healthy lives and healthy institutions possible.

While research findings and anecdotal evidence give credence to this claim, perhaps the most compelling reason I argue that holy friends are necessary for sustainability and flourishing is that this truth has been borne out over and over in my own life. My holy friends keep me alive. They know me. They love me. They root me in God's ongoing love story with creation. They tell me the truth. They hold space for me. They help me see a future I could never see on my own. The faces and voices of each one who has spoken truth and goodness in unique and impactful ways run like silver threads through the tapestry of my life, pulling me forward, keeping me upright, and pointing me over and over toward health and flourishing.

I do not claim to be an expert on holy friendships. I do, however, acknowledge the privileges I have that enable me not only to nurture my holy friendships but also to research and write about them. I am a white woman who grew up in a loving and faith-rooted family in which education was a priority. My spouse has a good job that allows him the flexibility to take care of all of the parenting and household duties so I can go visit friends. My children have figured out that when I spend time with my friends, I am a better mom, wife, and human. I have a job that gives me an ample amount of vacation time to see friends. I also look for opportunities to include my friends in collaborative work. All of these circumstances are privileges for which I am grateful and that have made this book possible.

In the chapters that follow are my thoughts on holy friendships: what they are, what they do, whom they might be with, where they come from, what prevents them, and what ripple effects they can have beyond individual relationships. That said, I cannot give you a clear and indisputable formula for finding, creating, or sustaining a holy friendship. Just as every person is unique, every holy friendship is unique too. I suspect the more you read, however, the more you will recognize the holy friendships you live and observe. And as you do, I hope your appreciation for their value expands to encompass what they truly are: relationships that sustain our ministries, enable us to flourish, and even preserve our lives.

Reflecting on holy friendships will be life-giving for sure, but the best parts of this book are the stories you will read. They are stories of some of the most beautiful, complex, challenging, hilarious, and helpful holy friendships I have had the privilege to live and observe. These stories are as sacred as the holy friends who live them.

A word about the stories: some of the most profound gifts my interviewees gave me in this process were their vulnerability and virtually immediate access to their stories and life lessons. I could write an entire book about each person's experience with holy friendships because each is so rich, multilayered, and diverse. I made every attempt to account for multiple kinds of diversity in my research, including gender identity, sexual orientation, race, ethnicity, geographic location, faith expression, vocational identity, age, relationship status, culture, socioeconomic status, political affiliation, education, ability, values, and anything else I could possibly imagine making up the beauty of God's beloved community. Each and every one of these expressions of personhood shapes and nuances one's holy friendships, how they talk about them, and how I convey them to you. They are both deeply personal and, at the same time, can be co-opted by aggressive visible and invisible agendas and used as weapons of oppression and privilege.

In an effort to celebrate and affirm the diversity of God's beloved community represented in these pages, I am choosing to be selective in which identifying markers I reveal about each person. I am very aware that all parts of one's identity are important. At the same time, I want to leave enough space around each person for the Holy Spirit to spark your imagination about who this person might be in your world. Everyone in these pages is or was (may they rest in peace and rise in glory) a living, breathing human, and thanks be to God, no two are the same.

Sometimes identifying markers are slightly modified, mostly to protect the innocent. Occasionally, stories and conversations are condensed so I don't bore you with details. These amazing people brought their whole selves to these conversations with me, and that is a pure gift. Offering you snippets of them is my gift to you. I hope you will receive them and treat them with tenderness, grace, awe, and an openness to seeing them in God's ongoing story so that you, too, can find yourself there with your holy friends.

Acknowledgments

I am deeply grateful and eternally indebted to all the amazing leaders who gave me a glimpse into their holy friendships. These are your stories, your people. You are the leaders of the churches and institutions forging new paths and creating fresh ways to be a beloved community in an increasingly divided world. Thank you for trusting me.

Greg Jones and Dave Odom first gave me the vocabulary around holy friendships in "Strategy and Vision," a class in my doctor of ministry program at Duke Divinity School. The fact that cultivating and nurturing holy friendships were taught as strategies for human flourishing both blew my mind and stilled my heart. Then Greg and Dave offered me a job in an environment in which holy friendships are modeled, respected, valued, and encouraged. I'm still living my dream.

Many of the stories included in this book were first published in *Faith & Leadership*, an offering of Leadership Education at Duke Divinity. They were edited by Sally Hicks and Aleta Payne, who make me look good and take no credit for it. Speaking of editors, compiling these stories and writing this book was a tumultuous experience because the content is so deeply personal. However, finding out Beth Gaede would be retiring mere days after I submitted my manuscript was gutting. She saw potential in my work before I put pen to page. Beth, thank you for believing in this work, for sharing your stories, and for making me a significantly better writer than when we began working together.

I'm grateful to my parents, who were the first people to model friendship for me. My younger brothers—Jack, Brian, and Douglas—were my first and are my constant friends.

Mark, Ava, and Owen, my nuclear family, you have faithfully walked with me through many iterations of this work. Thank you for your patience. This book is in many ways a love story for you. My prayer is that you give and receive the love of holy friendship all the days of your life.

My holy friends, you know who you are. What we have is sacred. It is deeply formed in God's love. Thank you for loving me enough to help me validate my past, hold space for me today, and help me midwife a vision for the future that is far greater than anything I can ask or imagine.

I am particularly grateful to Amy, Chris, and Mandy, my dearest holy friends. I couldn't and wouldn't do this without you. Your wisdom is woven throughout these pages just as your love and support are the threads that complete the tapestry of my life. You make my life beautiful, challenging, fun, exciting, meaningful, and worthwhile. You embody the love of God to me in the most vulnerable and generous ways. Thank you, my holy friends, for flourishing with me.

INTRODUCTION

Somewhere in my parents' attic, there is a picture of me at about four years old sitting on one end of a metal seesaw. My grin matches that of Erica, the little girl perched on the other end of the seesaw. My mom says Erica and I were inseparable best friends. But if I search my memory, the only thing I remember about Erica is a faded image of her standing in a small, crowded kitchen while her mother made us homemade tortillas over a smoking hot plate. I can still smell them. They were soft and tasted like heaven. How could we have been best friends when the only memory I can summon is one of tortillas?

A few years later, I graduated to several sets of friends: friends at school, friends from church, and friends in the neighborhood. I attended a small school that drew students from all over the county, so school friendship activity was confined to school hours or the occasional sleepover on weekends. I saw church friends every Sunday and Wednesday. Because my neighborhood was a big self-contained circle, my friends and I had the run of the neighborhood and went from house to house as we pleased, usually returning home just in time for dinner. If I needed to be found, a sibling would come looking for me, or a parent would start calling the usual hangouts.

Sometimes my neighbor friends and I would have disagreements and take a break from playing together. Seldom did our parents or teachers intervene. There were rarely quarrels among the friends at church because we weren't together often enough to become irritated with one another. And the school was very strict. Corporal punishment with a long wooden paddle was the preferred method of correction, so we kept our tiffs to a minimum, determined to make sure a teacher would not notice.

In the end, it was the neighborhood that became the training ground for friendship. We knew who all the potential playmates were, so if we weren't getting along with a friend, we practiced weighing the pros and cons of resolution versus relocation to another house in the neighborhood. Of course, the worst-case scenario was alienation to the point that we had only siblings left for playmates. Thus, by necessity throughout our elementary school years, we figured out how to make relationships work.

As my motley neighborhood crew aged, neighborhood, magnet, and private schools divided us. For the most part, we conformed to the social constraints of our chosen schools. There remained, however, an underlying acknowledgment that we came from the same place and shared the same experiences—watching the firefighters pull one of us out of the wet cement of a construction site; outrunning an angry, exhausted adult when they discovered we'd used the overstuffed yard waste bags at the end of their driveway for target practice; and sharing and keeping childhood secrets under penalty of death or social ruin.

Families moving and our progressing into our later teenage years sent us all off in different directions. A handful of us remain connected on social media, and occasionally one of us will comment on a picture showing a mini version of our friend in the face of their child, calling us back to the memories. I take comfort, and I know those friends do too, in remembering those simpler times when we were figuring out what it meant to be human, to be friends, and to be in community together.

College at a small liberal arts school in the South taught me two primary lessons about friendship: (1) there is great value in being friends with people different from you, and (2) most eighteen- to twenty-two-year-olds have no idea who they are or how to befriend themselves, resulting in tumultuous times when they try to figure out how to be friends with one another. Looking back, my most meaningful friendships blossomed with people who pushed me to figure out who I was coming to be. Sometimes this happened in beautiful and productive ways; sometimes those learning opportunities were painfully memorable.

I attended seminary for a three-year master of divinity program immediately following college at another small school in a different southern state. This is where I first experienced what I would call young adult friendship. I made a handful of dear friends whom I still treasure today. I met my spouse, Mark, in my second year, and we married three years later. I was nurtured, encouraged, challenged, and affirmed by these friends and some incredibly wise teachers, and it was through these friendships that I found my vocation.

My seminary friends helped me articulate the ways my faith defines how I live, love, and work in the world. They watched me question and release my rigid, dualistic ways of seeing the world and my faith. They stayed with me as I waded into new ways of understanding God. This hard, soul-searching work drew me farther from the safety of my upbringing and pushed me deeper into an ocean with

more questions than answers, but I learned I can brave
that deep and wide ocean if I'm not alone.

In those three years, my friends and I learned, traveled, laughed, loved, lost, and suffered together. Some
lost babies or parents. Some fell in love; others fell out
of love. Ongoing church and denominational politics
provoked ongoing passionate conversations about polity,
autonomy, inclusivity, and inerrancy—topics seminarians like to discuss late into the night, experiences that
forge lifelong friendships.

In early marriage, friendship was a serious challenge
for me. We moved to Chapel Hill, North Carolina, where
Mark had gone to college and still had friends. I was a
stranger. We were both in school and lived in a base-
ment apartment with barely enough aboveground space
to count as legal windows. We called it "the mole hole."
The darkness of the environment, the challenge of a new
marriage and no friends, a rigorous degree program, and
each of us working at least two jobs to make ends meet
sent me into deep depression and anxiety. Adding to this
hard season, Mark's father's Parkinson's disease caused a
further decline in his body, and then lymphoma began to
take over. Weekends and the summer were spent with his
family three hours north in Virginia, making it hard to
sink roots anywhere.

During one of those trying semesters, Meg was one of
my students who was particularly gifted and a lot of fun to
have in class. As a teaching assistant, I couldn't cultivate
a friendship with her. This made me sad, because I sensed
we had a lot in common, and I needed a friend desper-
ately. As soon as the semester was over, she approached
me and said, "This was a great class, and I loved working
with you. But I want you to know I will not be taking any

more classes in which you are a teaching assistant." I was taken aback. She continued, "I've decided we are going to be friends, so you can't assign my grades. So when are we going to lunch?"

Meg and I quickly became friends. She walked with me through a challenging season in a new family system after I married. Over the years, we have gone in and out of each other's lives through jobs, marriages, kids, and vocational shifts. She is still the kind of friend for whom I will always pick up the phone, and I know she will do the same for me.

After that degree program, Mark and I needed "real jobs." We moved to Williamsburg, Virginia, where Mark became the associate pastor of a church, and I commuted to work at the seminary we'd first attended in Richmond. Spending ninety minutes in the car each day cut out a lot of potential social time, as did my maintaining and cultivating friendships in Richmond while Mark built a community in Williamsburg.

This was where we began to learn about the strange dynamic of being friends with parishioners. In this season, I developed amazing relationships with role models—women ten to fifteen years older than I was who helped me figure out marriage, having children, working, and friendship.

Jennifer taught me never to write something down unless I am comfortable owning it for the rest of my life (before social media even existed).

Audrey, a treasured coworker, modeled for me a kind of grace I strive to embody to this day. In the midst of great pain, loss, betrayal, and conflict in our work environment, she maintained her sense of self-worth and taught me how to behave with professional dignity.

The Vegas Girls taught me about adult female friendship. The six of us worked together at a large retirement community. Alongside work challenges, we navigated relationships, parents, children, partners, and the ever-elusive work-life balance. The name Vegas, as you can imagine, came about because what we talked about at lunch every day stayed confidential among us. Friendship with these women for eight years made up some of the most exhausting, most challenging, funniest, and happiest years of my life. When I think of friendship, I will forever think of Vegas.

While working toward a doctor of ministry for Christian institutional leadership at Duke Divinity School, I first heard the term *holy friends* in a class with Dr. L. Gregory Jones. His language and framework for holy friendship put into perspective all the formational friendships that had gotten me this far. He defined holy friends as those who name the sins we have come to love, affirm the gifts we are afraid to claim, and help us dream the dreams we otherwise would not dream. His definition resonated deep in my soul. He encouraged me to dig deeper, to look harder, and to rethink his idea. With that permission, I did, and holy friendship came to mean something slightly different as I struggled to articulate what I meant. The process of finding new words changed me, and it did indeed change my definition of holy friendship: mutual and sacred relationships deeply formed in God's love.

Out of my doctoral cohort, which began as a diverse group of fifteen mostly midlife interdenominational and interdisciplinary Christian leaders, organically emerged a small group of six of us who formed a writing covenant group to finish our dissertations. In the five years it took for all of us to finish, we developed a lovely bond of holy friendship animated by calls and texts with news, crises, celebrations, and challenges. We shared resources, family stories, church conflicts, and most importantly, support.

While we were spread across the country, if two of us were in the same city, a meal and/or drinks were shared, followed by pictures in the group text. We FaceTime about every other month because we value literal face time, seeing one another, and catching up. These became "my people," living examples of the ideas I'd been learning.

In the past decade, I have intentionally cultivated a robust circle of holy friends. These individuals and I share a connection that binds us together regardless of how often we talk or share a cup of coffee. While some are closer than others, all of them are critical to my flourishing.

In each stage of my life, I needed different things from my friends and they from me. As I've aged, I've become clearer about what I need from my friends and what I just don't have time for. I'm more than twenty years into a life partnership with a good man who loves and challenges me. I'm trying to raise two teenagers to be decent, kind humans. I tenuously navigate relationships with aging parents. I have a job I love that enables me to connect to God and God's work in the world. The holy friends I hold close help me figure out how to do all of this better, more clearly and gently, and with more focus and fun, resulting in greater impact and a deeper sense of living into who God is calling me to be. These are the people with whom I seek out, cultivate, and nurture relationships. These holy friends see, know, and participate in my world; we help make one another better.

It's taken me forty-plus years. I know what I need in my friends. And best of all, I know what I need in my holy friends. This deep knowledge changes everything. It changes how I enter relationships and the way I budget my time and travel. Most importantly, identifying, seeking out, and nurturing holy friendships has profoundly changed the way I live, love, teach, write, parent, and exist in the world as I bear witness to the God who has extended the holiest hand of friendship I could ever imagine.

Finding the qualities and the people we need in holy friendships takes time. For me, it took tortillas, backyard clubs, high school drama, sorority sister scandals, mind-bending seminary experiences, anxiety, depression, loss, trauma, joy, and love to figure it out. My path is only one path. Yours will look different from mine. But I can assure you that every twist, turn, bump in the road, and unexpected detour is worth it when you figure out who you are, what you need, what you can offer, and what you can receive. Holy friends make life better, fuller, albeit more challenging at times; they are a precious glimpse of the reign of God.

Your story of friendship is holy too. And you can call your holy friends whatever you want to call them: Ride or dies. Besties. Soulmates. Anam cara. BFFs. Sisters. Brothers. Framily. Whatever that name may be, just please, for the sake of all that is holy . . . have them.

Jesus and Friendship

Having grown up steeped in the flannel board stories of evangelical Sunday school and daily Bible classes in school, I have wondered for years about Jesus's friendships. What kind of friend was he? The disciples were more than work colleagues who left their old lives behind to follow him in a new life of "fishing for people." They traveled, ate, stayed, learned, and lived together.

According to tradition and stories in the New Testament, Jesus had an inner circle among the disciples. While texts do not explicitly say Jesus chose Peter, James, and

John to be his closest friends or that they chose him, the relationship is implied because of their presence at specific events. The three were with Jesus when he raised Jarius's daughter from the dead (Mark 5:37; Luke 8:51), at the transfiguration (Mark 9; Matt 17; Luke 19), and in the garden of Gethsemane (Mark 14:33; Matt 26:37). They were with Jesus in a moment of glory and honor on the mount and in extreme grief in the garden. While Peter's life story is blotted with moments of weakness and betrayal, he is also the "rock" on which Jesus trusts the church's beginnings. And James and John suffer and are martyred for their faith (Matt 20:22).

Mary Magdalene is present at many gatherings, including the crucifixion. While Scripture does not mention her as often or as favorably as the disciples, she is prominent among the women who are part of the inner circle of the Messiah. Luke 8:1–3 records, "Soon afterward he [Jesus] went on through one town and village after another, proclaiming and bringing the good news of the kingdom of God. The twelve were with him, as well as some women who had been cured of evil spirits and infirmities: Mary, called Magdalene, from whom seven demons had gone out, and Joanna, the wife of Herod's steward Chuza, and Susanna, and many others, who ministered to them out of their own resources." Luke also tells us that Mary Magdalene, Joanna, and Mary the mother of James are the ones who went after Jesus's crucifixion to put spices on his body and discovered the tomb was empty (Luke 24:10). These faithful women traveled with and took part in Jesus's everyday ministry of loving God and loving one another.

The story of Mary, Martha, and Lazarus in John 11 certainly connotes a close relationship. Twice the text says Jesus loved this family. When the sisters confront him about their brother's death, Jesus cries for the loss of his friend alongside the sisters, who felt his death in their very core. Jesus's weeping over Lazarus's passing shows a depth of care for Lazarus and his family that goes beyond a traditional friendship. The account suggests they may have been among Jesus's holy friends.

Thinking about Jesus and his friends helps me imagine his humanity. When we examine Jesus's relationships, we see that his life and ministry are deeply rooted in love—loving God and loving one's neighbor. He surrounds himself with people who share his values and vision for a more just world. God's divine plan to share God's love with the world in the embodied humanity of Jesus is manifest in Jesus's friendships and relationships. Sometimes, then, when we read stories about Jesus, it isn't clear who is a friend and who is a colleague or an acquaintance. The same is true in our lives. My spouse will refer to someone in a conversation as my friend, and I will search my brain trying to figure out to whom he is referring only to discover he means someone I met once and would not consider a friend.

One could make the argument that because the disciples called Jesus "Rabbi," he was in a hierarchical role over them as their teacher, thus making the relationship not mutual. However, Jesus is clear in John 15:12–17 (part of his Farewell Discourses), when he changes the metaphor of their relationship from master and servant to friends, that he wants a relationship of mutuality and vulnerability:

> This is my commandment, that you love one another as I have loved you. No one has greater love than this, to lay down one's life for one's friends. You are my friends if you do what I command you. I do not call you

servants any longer, because the servant does not know what the master is doing; but I have called you friends, because I have made known to you everything that I have heard from my Father. You did not choose me but I chose you. And I appointed you to go and bear fruit, fruit that will last, so that the Father will give you whatever you ask him in my name. I am giving you these commands so that you may love one another.

When a servant serves their master, there are clear roles and boundaries to follow. The relationship is hierarchical and transactional. One has privilege; the other serves. Each is dependent on the other but not in a mutually beneficial way. The servant-master metaphor is repeated throughout Scripture, which makes it an easy model for our relationship with Christ and others. And yet here, Jesus advocates for friendship. Friendship, as opposed to a servant-master relationship, is purposeful and requires constant nurturing. The friendship Jesus speaks of here is deeply rooted in conversation and a shared way of life rather than boundaries and expectations. We, as friends, are invited into conversation with God and God's Son. We are given a model of friendship characterized by intimate sharing, fidelity, and generous vulnerability. Friends are willing to lay down their lives for each other—which Jesus literally does, we learn four chapters later. Friends share with each other what they know, including, or perhaps especially, what they know from God. In doing so, Christ provides an example for our friendships. He offers a more personal and mutual model of relationship. Christ wants and advocates for friendship.

How to Use This Book

Somewhere I heard a marketing guru say, "People don't buy products; they buy a better version of themselves. They buy a story they want to participate in." I hope as you read the stories in these pages you find yourself longing for friendships like these, friendships that will nurture and sustain you and your ministry. These friendships will bring you closer to God and help you better emulate the love and ministry of Jesus.

In what's to come, you'll read how holy friendships have contributed to flourishing among Christian leaders and thriving communities. You can deduce practical advice about where to look for holy friends and how to develop them. As you read, you will also begin to identify holy friendships in your own life, discern ways to nurture and sustain them, and celebrate the potential within us all to cultivate holy friendships that make us stronger and that make the world stronger. Read along and see if any of this feels familiar, or even better, if it creates a longing in you that inspires you to seek out and strengthen holy relationships in your own life.

- You can discover what kind of holy friendships you need to better live into the person and leader God is calling you to be.
- You can look across your friendships and name the ones that are holy. Then you can sanctify them, set them apart from others, because they *are* different. You can learn how to protect them. Treasure them. Nurture them. Thank God for them.
- You can assess those with whom you have had seasonal holy friendships and celebrate their

unique and formative qualities. Remembering
them (re)places them on your radar when you
need them or they need you in the future.

- You can impact someone else's life with this
  book. If you know the love, challenge, support,
  and care of a holy friend, share this with someone else who may not have this language or these
  relationships.

- You can share stories about your holy friendships.
  The more we talk about them, the more normal-
  ized they will become, the more relationships will
  be nurtured, the healthier and more sustainable
  our beloved communities will become, and the
  closer earth will come to heaven.

The best, most transformative work is always done in
collaboration because God made us for community. Life
is so much fuller and more meaningful when we have at
least one holy friend with whom we are honest, authentic, accountable, and in regular contact. Someone who gets
who we are and why we do what we do is even better.

My experience teaching, talking with, and listening to
Christian leaders for more than twenty years has taught
me that holy friendships contribute to the flourishing of
Christian leaders and thriving communities. When you
are a healthy leader, you can lead others into health, and
the ripple effects of that health continue ad infinitum. Holy
friendships are among the most effective, stimulating, joyful, and worthwhile ways to experience this human journey and the challenge we're given to lead God's people.

1

Who Are They?

Exploring Definitions of Holy Friendship

Marcus hadn't heard from Scott in two weeks, which was odd. In their fifteen years of friendship, they rarely went a few days without a text, email, or call. Even a ridiculous GIF could communicate enough to keep a conversation going between them two hundred miles apart. When Marcus called, Scott answered on the first ring. His words tumbled out, his voice exasperated and exhausted:

> I know. You probably think I've dropped off the face of the earth. I should have called you, texted, something. It all happened so fast. A small faction of the church called for a vote of no confidence in my leadership after I mentioned in a sermon that getting vaccinated is a way we can love God and love our neighbors. The church had to follow due process, and most folks just wanted it over, so it was a whirlwind of activity. The vote was last night. Eighty percent of the membership supports me. I'm exhausted. I'm not even sure what the vote means in the grand scheme of things. I've been here most of my vocation, and I

thought I would retire here. I don't know which way is up anymore. The pandemic. The politics. The budget. It is all so much.

Marcus responded, "I'm so sorry. Wow. This is a lot. Let me just sit for a second before I say anything." He then texted his spouse and said he needed to visit Scott for a few days. Could they cover his duties with the house and their family? After about a minute, Marcus answered: "Scott, you need to get out of there. You can't think in that space. I can't imagine it feels safe. Do what you need to do to leave tonight and meet me halfway in Jonesboro. I'll get us rooms at the Hampton Inn. If you want to sleep for twenty-four hours, that is fine. But then we will eat at that great Italian place and figure out what happens next. Talk to Sonja. Throw some clothes in a bag. OK? I'll see you tonight."

Scott replied, "You are right. Thank you. That's exactly what I need. I can't think here. I'm sorry I didn't fill you in earlier. I should have. It's just been a nightmare."

Marcus cut him off: "Hey. No apologies. We are good. What matters right now is you. We'll figure this out together. This is what holy friends do for each other."

Holy friendships are mutual and sacred relationships deeply formed in God's love. Holy friends share all levels of friendship from casual chitchat (typically with deeper connections than in ordinary friendships) to ongoing discussions about a challenge one is working on to dark-night-of-the-soul conversations. In the story above, Marcus and Scott are committed to each other's well-being, and they prioritize caring for the other's spiritual, mental, and physical health. They see each other as vital contributors to bearing witness to God's work in the world. To learn more about their friendship and many more in the pages to follow, let's explore the key words in my definition of holy friendship.

Anthropologist and evolutionary psychologist Robin Dunbar defines friendship in his book *Friends* as "a two-way process that requires both parties to be reasonably accommodating and tolerant of each other, to be willing to spare time for each other."[1] Definitions of friends can be profoundly personal, as *friend* connotes different levels of relationships to those experiencing them. A friend can be anyone from a casual acquaintance to someone for whom we would lay down our life (John 15:13). Generally, a friend is someone we know, we enjoy spending time with, with whom we share at least one common interest that draws our attention toward one another, and in whom we have a minimum amount of trust. Reciprocity is significant to friendships. Friends delight in each other and consistently show up for each other in good and challenging seasons.

Holy and *sacred* are overlapping terms that support each other. A holy friendship consists of more than a pair of friends. God is at the center of it; thus, it is set apart, privileged, and protected. A holy friendship is different from an ordinary friendship because it is held in God's love and part of God's bigger, ongoing story in the world.

The sacredness of holy friendships means they are different from our relationship with the person we talk to regularly at the bus stop, our neighbor over the fence, or our favorite cashier at the corner store. When we connect with a holy friend, the dopamine that hits our brain is different from our body's reaction when we see other friends because we instantly recognize, appreciate, and affirm in this intimate relationship our trust, sense of accountability, and desire for each other's flourishing as we bear witness to God's love. We know we are in a safe space. We know we are in the presence of not only our holy friend but also God's love and care through them.

Society tends to regard things that are holy and sacred as serious and solemn, and holy friendships can be both. They can also be full of light, beauty, rest, renewal, comfort, joy, compassion, and delight. Some of the most sacred moments of my life have been filled with tears of laughter in the presence of my holy friends. My cheeks ache and my stomach muscles almost burst from all of the hilarity, joy, and silliness when I fully relax into time with my holy friends. We know we are loved. We are more than enough. There is no competition, only support and mutual delight in one another's flourishing. These are the moments, people, and relationships that sustain me.

What do I mean when I say holy friendships are deeply formed in God's love? First John 4:8 reminds us that God is love. God's love is embodied in Jesus Christ and God's divine image (*imago Dei*) within each human. We are called to exemplify God's love for one another. As Jesus tells the Pharisees, the greatest commandment is to love God, our neighbors, and ourselves (Matt 22:37–39). We seek intimate and soulful connections with others who bear God's divine image and help us see that image in one another. Holy friends may not look different to the outside world. What sets them apart is that they have a larger purpose beyond the friendship itself: they help point both people toward God. Holy friends help us discover what 1 Timothy 6:19 calls "the life that really is life."

Holy friendships are mutual. The friends belong to each other, and they acknowledge that with the other. While the acknowledgment can be assumed or explicit, I encourage us to be explicit in our conversations about friendship for two reasons. First, having our feelings for another person verbally reciprocated feels good. Who doesn't want to hear they are loved, cared for, heard, and seen? Everyone wants to belong somewhere, to someone. Articulating what we mean to each other affirms our intuition about our friend and confirms we are both desiring holy friendship. Second, being explicit clarifies the intentions and expectations of the friendship so both friends are aware of the relationship's significance, enabling them to fully partake in the beauty, joy, fun, and challenge holy friendship brings.

I am often asked, "Do we actually have to say the words 'We are holy friends' to be holy friends? Can't we just know it?" I assume what is beneath that question is the cultural aversion to talking about feelings and a fear that the other person might not reciprocate the feelings or sentiment. My answer is, do what feels right for you and your holy friend, but if you don't talk about your friendship, I encourage you to think about why you don't. If talking about it feels weird, you might not be in a holy friendship, one in which you can be truly vulnerable and say anything. If you are hesitant that the friend might not reciprocate a holy friendship level of investment, you probably are not in a holy friendship.

Make It Weird

A meme circulated through social media: "Normalize telling your friends you love them. Tell them a lot. Make it
weird." The best memes go viral because they have a much
deeper meaning than a first reading suggests. I love everything about this meme.

Many of us lack the language to talk about our friendships because our social norms do not provide space to
verbalize their attributes and benefits. Sometimes we
think if we have to talk about something or label it, it
isn't valuable or real. We surmise that friendships are
supposed to exist, just be, without talking about them. In
reality, the opposite is true. We should be talking about
the things that are most important to us. If friendships are
important, we need to talk about them.

Let's talk about them. A lot. Let's make it weird.

Holy friends are comfortable talking about their friendship. While most of us don't talk often about the value and
idiosyncrasies of friendships, what I found in my research
is that most holy friends take great joy in verbalizing their
affection for each other. It is not embarrassing or silly. It is
affirming, life-giving, and fun! Many pairs of holy friends,
when they reflected with me on their friendship, found
they learned new things from old stories they recollected
with each other. They expressed mutual satisfaction and a
desire to talk about their friendship more often.

For some people, mutuality feels risky. Belonging to
someone else can feel out of control. Relationships in
which we feel like we have some control and can keep

people at arm's length feel safer. We prefer transactional relationships, which are more likely to have clear boundaries defining what each person brings to the friendship and can expect from it. Holy friendships are not transactional; each friend willingly gives to and receives from the other out of love for each other and love for God.

Within most traditional churches, a pastor is called or appointed and paid to lead the congregation. The nature of a pastor's role places them in a position of power over the congregation, even when a congregation willingly follows a pastor's lead. Similarly, when a Christian leader is paid for the services they are trained to offer a community, the relationship between the leader and the community is transactional. Even though pastors and congregations may enter mutual contracts of employment and deeply care for one another, friendships between pastors and congregants cannot be truly mutual, because the transactional and hierarchical nature of the relationship cannot be ignored. We will discuss this limitation in more detail in chapter 7, when we talk about who our holy friends are not.

I am often asked to help leaders discern whether a particular relationship they have "counts" as a holy friendship. Some will ask, "Can I have a holy friendship with someone who isn't a Christian? Who is an atheist or an agnostic?" My response is always more questions: "Do you think you are in a holy friendship? What about my definition of holy friends is giving you pause?" It is not for me to decide what is holy, sacred, or mutual for someone else or their friends. I offer my definition and corresponding examples and stories with the hope of raising questions and adding to an ongoing conversation about what contributes to the flourishing of pastors and Christian leaders.

Let's Talk about Friendship

In my research for this book, I began interviews with pairs of holy friends in the same way: with a riff on *The New-lywed Game*. I gave each person a stack of note cards. Without showing the other their cards, they wrote their answers to the following questions. When I interviewed Mateo and Celena, Mateo's cards read,

- What do you bring to this friendship?
- What does Celena bring to this friendship?
- When did you know Celena would be someone holy/unique/special in your life?
- Tell me a story about when something happened and your first thought was that you had to talk to Celena.

The friends would take turns sharing their answers with each other. There were surprises, tears, and affirmations. This exercise created an intimate space for the holy friends.

Countless times, when we reached the end of the interview, one of the friends would say, "Why don't we ever talk like this? This felt amazing to share and to receive. We are always so busy *being* friends. We talk about other important things, but we don't talk about our friendship. We need to do this again."

Reflecting on my holy friendships and recounting our stories has helped me articulate my definition of holy friendships: mutual and sacred relationships, deeply formed in God's love. My friend Penny and I rarely end a call without one of us saying, "I couldn't do life without you. I love you." The other responds, "It is what we do for each other. I love you too." In these few words, we acknowledge and reinforce the significant roles we play in each other's lives. We mutually validate the work we put into nurturing our holy friendship. My friend Kit is one of those people who exudes the love of God in everything they do. While they may tire of hearing me, I remind them of and express gratitude for the example they set for me. They, in turn, regularly remind me, especially if I am disparaging myself, of the image of God in me and the way God is using me in their life and in the world. Holy friends mutually affirm, challenge, and encourage each other because they know their friendship is not just about them; it is about how God is working through them and loving God's creation.

2

HOW DO THEY FIT IN MY LIFE?

Mapping Friendships

"How do you decide which people to say 'I love you' to?" my son asked when he was around ten years old.

"Why do you ask?" I replied. He continued, "Sometimes you say it when you are getting off the phone, and sometimes you don't. Like, you always say it to Diana and Clara. And you say it to Max and James, so I know it's not just a girl thing. I know about Oma and Bapa [his grandparents]. I'm trying to figure out which friends you say it to and which friends you don't."

With my heart bursting that he was trying to use words to talk about his feelings, I responded, "I say I love someone because I mean it. I have loved the people you mention for a long time. Sometimes we are talking about something hard or that hurts, and they need to be reminded that they are loved and worthy of love. Sometimes I say it out of habit because, with them, it is always true—like when we are leaving the house and we shout 'Love you!' to whoever is staying home. I try to say it to people whenever I feel it because I don't think we say it enough. The expectations people have for what is or isn't normal in a conversation make us hesitant to express our feelings. So I guess my answer is, if I feel it, I say it."

I paused to see if I answered his question to his satisfaction.

"Is there someone you want to tell that you love them?" I tentatively asked.

He responded quickly: "Yeah, Lawson. He's my best friend and has been for three years. He's like my brother. We tell each other everything, and no matter what, we'll always be friends. So I'm just wondering, are there rules or something that only adults say it, or how does it work?"

"You can say it to whoever you want, whenever you want. They are your feelings. Just know that my friends don't always say it back. Most of the time they do. And sometimes we are in a hurry or one of us gets cut off. So if Lawson, or anyone else, doesn't say it back, it doesn't mean they don't love you too. It may just mean it wasn't the right moment to say it. We don't say it so someone will say it back. We say it because we mean it."

I love his question: Are there rules? Sometimes I wish there were. They could clarify some awkward situations. Rules could help us understand some of the mysteries of relationships. On the other hand, if there were rules, they would inevitably exclude certain people and relationships. So we are left to figure out how often and to whom our "I love you"s belong in our complicated, messy, cruel, beautiful world through trial and error with other humans who are just as uncertain. In the absence of rules to help us make sense of relationships and how to articulate our feelings, we can turn to the social sciences for adaptive tools and frameworks to help us think about those whom we like, love, and live among.

Social scientist Marc Dunkelman's 2014 book *The Vanishing Neighbor* maps social constellations and relationships with concentric rings as a tool to examine the declining sense of community in America today. Working from the inside out, our inner core includes intimate relationships such as with a partner, children, maybe parents, and dearest friends. The first ring holds those we consider fairly close to us. These may be longtime friends, people we talk to at least once a week, and those we could call in an emergency. The middle ring is home to familiar but not close contacts, such as coworkers, extended family, neighbors, friends from childhood, and those on our intramural soccer team. This ring is what Americans consider to be one's "community." The third or outer ring is for tangential or transactional relationships, such as with your regular

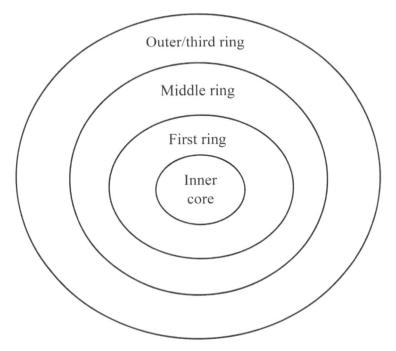

Figure 2.1 Dunkelman's map of social engagement

Amazon delivery person, the receptionist at your doctor's office, and random Facebook "friends." These relationships are often rooted in a single shared interest or experience; we know them but are not close to them.

In a similar vein, Robin Dunbar recently expanded his research on "Dunbar's number," the idea he proposed in the 1990s that the average individual can "know" 150 people, have fifteen close friends, and have no more than five in their inner circle / family / close companions. He now believes the typical human has "five close friends, fifteen best friends, fifty good friends, and 150 just friends."[1] He has added additional circles to his model and claims the average individual has five hundred acquaintances, can match 1,500 names and faces (known names), and can recognize five thousand faces (known faces).[2]

When we combine Dunkelman's social rings and Dunbar's circles and numbers, we can create a helpful map (figure 2.3) of our social ecosystem. We can look holistically at how we relate to people and specifically at who our holy

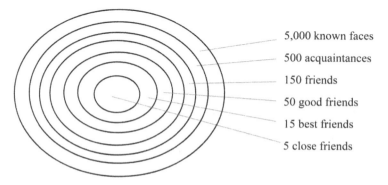

Figure 2.2 Dunbar's social circles

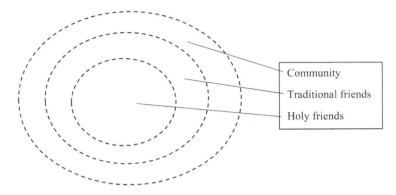

Figure 2.3 My relational ecosystem

friends are. Figure 2.3 shows how I map my ecosystem with a mashup of Dunkelman's and Dunbar's work.

The outer ring holds my community. These are people I recognize and casual acquaintances. I might see these people from afar on a regular basis, but I do not know them well enough to exchange more than pleasantries. This is where I place the parents of my children's friends, the owners of my dog's favorite canine friends (because we all remember the dogs' names much more quickly than we remember their owners'), folks I see at the gym or pool, and the like.

The second ring is where I list my traditional friends. These are people I might have lunch with every once in a while, my neighbors, people I take book recommendations from, and colleagues at work. We are familiar with each other, but we do not experience the vulnerability or sacredness of a holy friendship.

My holy friends are in the inner ring. These are people with whom I share mutual and sacred relationships deeply formed in God's love. These relationships necessitate a more significant level of intimacy, mutuality, and nourishment than with ordinary friends, thus they will be smaller in number.

I do not equate holy friends with Dunbar's close, best, or good friends or assign optimal numbers for each category. The number of people on your map is deeply contextual and personal. The map of an introvert in an isolated community will look quite different from that of an extrovert in a well-connected environment. Age, personality, race, gender, ethnicity, and other factors play a role in the way each person develops relationships, thus everyone's map and the way we label our circles will look different.

Flourishing comes from the quality of the relationships in our first two circles. I know pastors and other Christian leaders who are thriving with one holy friend, a handful of traditional friends, and large communities. Some leaders are thriving in small communities with ten holy friends and more than thirty friends they have collected over the years. One of my favorite leaders has one holy friend, just a few friends, and a vast community.

Those familiar with Dunbar's work will notice that figure 2.2 is missing the innermost circle. Dunbar says this circle has one and a half persons in it, signifying our most intense, intimate relationships—romantic partners, for example. How can a person have half of a friend? Dunbar writes, "Half the people have two of these special friends and half only have one. Women have two (a romantic partner and a Best Friend Forever, who is usually another girl), but men only have one (either a romantic partner or a drinking buddy, who is obviously male) because they can't manage both at the same time."[3] While Dunbar's tone comes with a bit of stereotypical jest, nonetheless, his research is solid.

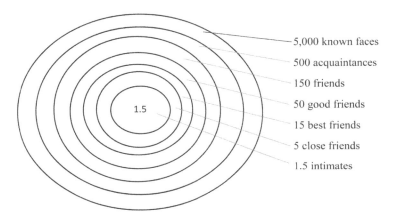

Figure 2.4 Dunbar's complete circles

I introduce Dunbar's innermost circle separately from the rest of his circles because some people have a few holy friendships with whom we share a profound connection. They are more intimate than others. I have three holy friends who are consistently closest to me, alongside my immediate family. I think of them as my chosen family. They are the people I talk with and text the most. They are the first ones I go to for advice, for confession, and to laugh, cry, and rant. We walk alongside each other through the major and minute details of our lives.

You may have a few holy friends who are closer than others. Mapping your friends is for your benefit, not to prove or validate anyone's relationship status. You determine who your holy friends are. You determine who goes on your map.

Where Does My Family Go on My Map?

Lakisha is a third-generation pastor. She knows not only what it is like to be a pastor's kid but what it is like to be a pastor's kid of pastors' kids. Growing up, she remembers her two sisters filling many of the social needs and expectations that would typically be filled by friends. Her family, like many clergy families, lived their lives in a fishbowl, on display for the church and community. Also, because of the high relational nature of their church, she was reared to be wary of people who wanted to get close to the pastor's family to acquire power or influence.

Lakisha immediately thinks of her sisters when she thinks of holy friends. She has pastoral colleagues who grew up in different contexts and might not think of their family in the same way.

Whether you choose to put family members on your map is up to you.

Our Changing Friendship Maps

While a friendship map can help us understand our relationships, our maps change over time. Notice that the rings of my friendship maps are not constructed of solid lines. The permeability of the rings reflects the fact that friends move in and out of the circles as each person grows and changes. There is no pride or shame associated with movement between the circles. Movement happens because life happens. We develop and mature, and our friendships change. Sometimes our friendships are strengthened with time and challenges. Other times friendships fade or are cut off. The permeability of the circles allows for this natural movement.

In the introduction, I mentioned incredible people who will always be my holy friends. Even though we claim each other as holy friends, however, our friendships have changed. We lived through a significant experience, and they were important holy friends in my life for that season. Audrey taught me how to love and leave an institution with dignity and grace. We stay in touch and see each other when we can. We text and email as occasions inspire us. We recently connected over her daughter and son-in-law trying to relocate somewhere near me, and I instantly became invested in their move because of my timeless love and respect for Audrey. Just knowing she is in Maine, being amazing at her job and anything else she puts her mind to, makes me feel happy and close to her. We can reconnect and be exactly who we need to be for each other at any moment and in any season. Seeing her on my map reminds me of our shared history and care for each other. Simply reading her name there affirms how much we have grown and offers hope for who we are still becoming. The permeability of our friendship circles affirms that we make the space for our holy friendship to change alongside our personal growth.

While it would be lovely to think that friendships always deepen and people consistently move toward the center of one's map, that is unfortunately not the reality. I've been a part of a small group of five Christian leaders who loved and respected one another for seven years. We frequently verbally affirmed and expressed gratitude for our holy friendships. We texted weekly, if not more often. We had frequent video calls and never lacked conversation, laughter, or mutual support. Because we were holy friends as I was beginning my research, together we developed some of the language in this book.

In the middle of what appeared to be a benign text thread, Nate misinterpreted something. Before any of the others had an opportunity to respond, Nate fired off multiple accusatory texts that took everyone else by surprise. Naturally, as holy friends do, we responded with apologies and requests for explanations and conversation. It took Nate a while to respond, and when they did, they said they needed time. We each took turns initiating contact through the group text and individually inviting conversation over several months. The months turned into years. Nate stopped responding.

When I was reflecting on what happened with Chase, another member of the group, he expressed what the other two of us were feeling in the liminal space of Nate's silence: "This isn't how it is supposed to go. This isn't what holy friends do. When one of us is ticked, we address it together. Be ticked in community with us. Don't just leave. They are better than this. We are better than this."

Maybe by the time you are reading these pages, this story will have a different ending. I hope so. Holy friendships need mutuality. We can't make Nate be in relationship with us, although we have continued to be in relationship without them. We can keep the door open, though, and we can pray for whatever it is that needs to happen and hope for reconciliation and reunion.

Such healing is possible. My friend Ana experienced something similar. She and a group of ten other women met weekly throughout seminary, rotating through the hospitality of one another's homes. They didn't need a topical agenda. Their vocations and classes and the intensity of seminary life provided more conversation fodder than they would ever need. The women came to rely on one another for mutual support, encouragement, and accountability. Their friendship made their seminary experience more formational and enjoyable.

Midway through their final year in the program, one of the women addressed the others in a way that felt out of character for her and outside the common practice of the group. She made what the others experienced as angry accusations, and she used hurtful language to describe the group and the relationships within it. Her words inflicted great pain, Ana recalls. Everyone felt confused and disoriented. The group fell apart. The women finished seminary and went on to serve in various places of ministry throughout the country. They kept their distance for more than thirty years.

When the Covid-19 pandemic exacerbated feelings of isolation and loneliness for seemingly everyone, one of the women recognized that she needed community. She wanted to be with people she knew and who knew her. She took a risk and reached out to the women in the group (save the one) and invited them to a Zoom gathering. Ana recalls that after everyone had logged on to the first Zoom call, the group members chatted as if no time had passed. They leaned into the foundation of trust, love, and care they had built a generation earlier. Their holy friendship was renewed. They continue to gather for two hours once a month, and as in the first season of their holy friendship, they never run out of ways to support and encourage one another.

These examples of holy friendships changing raise this question: Do holy friendships end? While I will not speak for others in the group Nate was part of, I think they and

I are no longer holy friends. The mutuality was broken
when they stopped responding to my (and the others') invitations to talk about the source of their discontent with us.
The pain of the broken relationship was such that I needed
closure. And eventually, I had to accept what they were
communicating to me: there was nothing left. I needed to
move on so I could invest that emotional energy elsewhere
in my life. As I said earlier, maybe my answer will be different someday. I'd like to think it will be. But for today,
I assume the relationship has ended.

Sometimes the movement between the circles of our maps
occurs because a holy friendship is stronger, more intense,
or more necessary for a particular season. The opposite is
also true. Think about plants in a garden. In some seasons,
they might have beautiful blooms, and in others, the plants
are dormant. Spells of dormancy enable us to nourish other
life-giving sources, trusting that the mutuality of holy friendships will remain through both fallow and fruitful seasons.
Seasonal holy friends, which I believe include Ana and her
friends, are close enough and removed enough from our
daily lives to be able to move in and out of the everyday fray
as we need one another.

I have some seasonal holy friends with whom I hav-
en't connected in years who I still count within my holy-
friendship circle. To say we haven't "needed each other"
sounds harsh, even though it is true. However, I trust in
the mutuality of our holy friendship and rest in the confidence and assurance of our shared history that when the
time is right, we will circle back and be again present with
each other because our bond is sacred and rooted in God's
love.

Life Changes Prompt Friendship Changes

Judith's close college friend Abby married and immediately began having children. Judith remembers intentionally recognizing that Abby had multiple life changes happening at once. She knew Abby didn't have much time, energy, or effort to contribute to their friendship, even if Abby wanted to.

Judith was self-aware enough to know that reciprocity mattered to her. She didn't like always being the one to call or initiate coffee dates or lunch. But because Abby was important to her, she made the decision to carry the weight of their friendship in that season. Abby was grateful and knew this was a concession and act of love from Judith.

Eventually, Abby got into a groove with her new life as a wife and mother and was able to contribute more time and energy to their friendship. Weathering the season together made it manageable for both holy friends.

I have experienced this seasonality most clearly when a holy friend is evolving through a major life change: having a child, losing a parent, changing jobs, weathering a financial crisis, moving to a new home, or dealing with a significant health diagnosis. In these seasons, they may not be able to show up for me in exactly the ways I need. Similarly, while I can be present and care for them, I may not have the kind of experience or expertise that would be most helpful to them. Foreseeing these kinds of situations enables us to find support elsewhere and offer our holy friends love and care specific to their capacities and needs. Verbally acknowledging these significant seasons rather than pulling back or ghosting them can be a gift to holy friends. We mark the seasons of the year. Perhaps it is equally important to mark when our friendships grow and change. We can do this through a conversation, a card, or something that shows you notice a shift in a relationship important to you as you trust that the holy friendship will find a new equilibrium.

The Value of Mapping Friendships

Mapping our relationships using Dunbar's and Dunkelman's rings and circles is intended to be a reflective exercise that over time can help us notice shifts in the types of support we need and provide in our relationships with our holy friends in different seasons of our lives. It helps us reflect on who we are in relationship with at any given time and consider the quantity and quality of our friendships. The map inspires gratitude to those with whom we have shared special seasons. It enables us to evaluate what we need to change in our relationships to flourish.

Gracie found mapping her relationships insightful when she was experiencing major transitions in several areas of her personal and professional life. Her map revealed holy friends who had been particularly helpful in previous seasons of her life with whom she needed to reconnect. Some, she remembered, had experience with transitions similar to the ones before her. Upon reflection, she realized she might feel close to fewer people at the moment because so much of her energy is going to starting a business and caring for a loved one with cancer. She's grateful for the mapping exercise's affirmation of her holy friends' abiding presence throughout the ebbs and flows of her life, especially because she feels like she is currently in an ebbing state. She looks forward to a new season in which she can reverse the flow and better engage her holy friends.

Mapping our friends can provide a framework for critical questions about the people we as pastors and Christian leaders rely on for support, affirmation, accountability, and mutual flourishing. We might ask questions such as these:

- Do my holy friends have a "type"? Are they primarily of one gender, race, ethnicity, orientation, age, or another identifier? What might this tell me about who I trust and who trusts me?
- Did my holy friendships originate in a particular season of my life? Seminary? Early adulthood? Midlife?
- How is each of my holy friends different from and similar to me? How are they different from one another?
- Who has fallen off or faded from my map and why?
- Are there specific qualities I have to see in a person in order to have a holy friendship with them?
- What conditions have to be present for me to develop additional holy friendships?
- What role do holy friendships play in my family, church/organization, and community?
- To what and to whom do I most clearly attribute my flourishing?

Reflecting on questions like these can raise awareness about who we are as leaders and the roles holy friends play in our health and well-being. It might be helpful to map your holy friends with them to look for overlaps in your friendships, ministries, and networks. You might find ways to strengthen ties you didn't realize were there.

As you reflect on your circles and who is in them, try to refrain from judgment. Your map is as different and unique as you are. You know the kind of care and support you need to flourish. My hope is that this tool will help you discern what you have, what you need, and who you are to others.

3

WHAT DO THEY DO?

Holy Friendships over Time

As my husband completed a phone call, my daughter astutely said, "Clayton is one of your holy friends."

"Yes," he replied. "We've known each other for more than thirty years, and we have been present in some really significant moments in each other's lives. What we have is holy. But how do you know he is my holy friend?"

Ava smiled and said, "Because your laugh is different when you talk with him. It's a full-body laugh that comes from a place deep in your soul. When I hear you laugh with Clayton, I know nothing else in the world matters to you. You are totally present in that moment. That kind of laughter can only come from a pure relationship that has stood the test of time."

Holy friends walk alongside us in our journeys in such a way that we experience life differently with them. In their company, our bodies, minds, and spirits can relax into a sacred and trusted space so powerful that it can, in my husband's case, change the sound of his voice and affect the way he laughs. Just as loving God changes the way we live and love in the world, so do our holy friends.

They are faithful companions in our past, present, and future.

Holy friends bless each other with support, challenges, affirmations, vulnerability, empathy, and love. Holy friends don't need to know every detail of each other's lives. They do, however, know enough of each other's history, significant goals, and current goings-on to bear witness to each other's lives. With time and experience, we can recognize a pattern in what we do for our holy friends and what they do for us. In their simplest form, holy friends support each other in three primary ways. Holy friends validate our past, hold space in the present, and help us midwife a vision for the future.

Validating the Past

Holy friends help us see the world through God's eyes so we can locate ourselves in the larger story of God. One of the ways we do this for each other is by validating the other's past and helping renarrate and reframe the harmful stories we tell ourselves. Too often, our self-understanding is distorted by sin, self-deception, and our participation in destructive mindsets and practices. Everyone has recordings from the past that seem to play in constant loops. We allow negative voices that often no longer apply to our current context to infiltrate our thoughts and actions. We hesitate, question the voices, and wonder why they continue to haunt us. Holy friends hear those stories—even if they were not present when they were first recorded—validate our feelings, and when needed, offer a counternarrative.

What Do They Do?   43

After a particularly hard season in which I was painfully betrayed by an organization I had invested in, I was talking with a holy friend about my trepidation about committing my time, energy, and gifts to a new organization. "I'm really starting to like this place," I told him. "I love the mission, and our values align. The people seem to genuinely care and want me to thrive. I just don't know if I can trust it. I can feel myself holding back. I keep waiting for the other shoe to drop."

He waited a pregnant pause, for which he is notorious, then said, "You've done the research on this new organization. Everything I have heard you talk about sounds positive, healthy, and hopeful. I think you should trust that. The other shoe is going to drop. It always does. And shoes are manageable. You can survive shoes. What happened to you in the last place wasn't a shoe. It was having the rug ripped out from underneath you."

With that simple metaphor shift, my hesitancy eased. In those few sentences, he gave me several generous gifts:

- He validated my painful experience.
- He reminded me that I can survive painful institutional challenges and come out stronger.
- He affirmed my instincts and the work I did to find a place of health and hope.
- He reminded me that no organization is perfect.
- He helped me picture how the two situations were dramatically different.

I also heard him say I needed to offer myself some grace. Surviving a rug being ripped out from underneath me was painful. It wasn't my fault, and I couldn't have seen it coming. Shoes, on the other hand, drop. Sometimes I see them falling, and other times I don't. Either way, I feel better moving forward knowing I will eventually be holding some shoes, the result of which I will survive and because of which I might even thrive at some point.

Poet and conversational leadership strategist David Whyte describes this reframing practice in what he calls "the beautiful and disturbing question: What is the story we need to stop telling?" Whyte goes on to say, "In order to change, in order to grow, we have to have room and space to do so. But so often we are filled inside with old, tired stories—narratives about what we've been told we can do and can't do."[1] Holy friends can sense when our old, tired stories are limiting us. Whyte identifies this as the point when we become sick of ourselves. He says this is a good sign because it is only then that we can truly hear our holy friends beckoning us to something more, something better, something more Christlike than what is holding us back.

Holy friends validate our past and help us reframe our old stories to reorient us toward God's love. They redirect our perspectives and reframe unhelpful memories so we can learn from our past and live into fresh and healthier versions of our vocation. They do this by offering alternative perspectives, reminding us that interpretations are not always set in stone and stories can be retold from different points of view, and inviting us to shift the way we behave in light of new discoveries and learning. Holy friends help set us free from what holds us back and walk alongside us into a healthier present and future.

Cultural anthropologist Marlon Hall has a powerful mantra he shares when he teaches a yoga class. Helping his students focus on the alignment of the body, mind, and spirit, he has his students repeat, "I am not my thoughts." Our negative thoughts can easily strip us of feelings of worthiness, love, hope, peace, or happiness. Holy friends sense this and name or, to use a biblical metaphor, "call out" the demons of negative self-talk and self-sabotaging thoughts and call us to a space where sin is brought to light. Once the negativity is revealed in the light of God's love and grace, we can renarrate our once painful stories, not to erase the pain, but to rewrite the ending with an emphasis on redemption. Holy friends see us in our pain, stick beside us, and guide us into new life where we record new mantras, reframe old memories, and tell stories of resilience and hope. Ultimately, holy friends are our story editors.

Validating our past and renarrating unhelpful stories about ourselves and others is some of the most vulnerable and brave work holy friends do for each other. We share our fears and failures, our hopes and dreams, and we reveal parts of ourselves few people ever see. This is the sacred space in which holy friends pull us, sometimes kicking and screaming, out of the past and into a more hopeful and healthy present and future filled with meaning and purpose.

I Need My People

Lauren, a pastor and denominational leader, describes her holy friendships like this:

This work would be impossible without them. I couldn't be the kind of clergy that I am without my holy friends. We are turning over tables, and that comes at a cost. Whether it is reputation, money, membership, emotional exhaustion and energy, feeling isolated, or whatever it is, there is a cost to the way we minister in the world. I don't know how to do it without having people I can trust to be vulnerable with, to be authentic with, to cuss with. I need my people who will listen, offer support, encouragement, words of affirmation, whatever it is in the moment. Otherwise, this pace, this ministry, this life is just impossible to sustain.

Holding Space in the Present

Most of the work my holy friends and I do for each other is some form of holding space in the present. "Holding space" means that the two holy friends agree to attentively listen to the other, reserve judgment, invite reflection, and accompany each other in a challenging conversation or experience. One leader explained, "My holy friends create a space where I can bring all of who I am. I don't feel like I need to wear any masks or be someone else to be accepted or received. They help me be vulnerable, especially when it is hard." In offering this vulnerable space for each other, holy friends create an environment in which both are spiritually, mentally, physically, and emotionally safe and accepted for who they are as children of God.

When holy friends hold space for each other, we focus our attention on what is and is not being said and how the Holy Spirit is moving in the stories and the space. We might be accountability partners, walk alongside each other in trauma, or reorient our attention away from our needs and wants to God's. Thanks to technology, holding space for a friend is not limited to in-person conversations— although for trauma and other intense discussions, it is highly preferred. We can hold space from afar through calls, videos, texts, messages, and mail.

My holy friend Jean and I have a code word for holding space for each other: *basket*. One of us will text the other and say, "I need you to hold my basket for about ten minutes. Will you let me know when you are available?" The reply lets the other know when to expect a call.

If I am the one who requested the basket, Jean will call me, and we have an intentionally one-sided conversation in which Jean holds space for me. Jean holds a metaphorical basket; I like to think of it as a large laundry basket. I spew out anything and everything on my mind in a run-on sentence, a cathartic rant. I am as vulnerable as I choose to be. She may let me know she is listening or make empathetic sounds like "Uh-huh," "Oh, wow," and "That sounds hard." She doesn't question my rationality or logic. She doesn't ask for more details. She listens without judgment and holds the basket while I dump in everything that is bothering me.

Holy Friends Help Us
Carry Heavy Things

A few weeks into the Covid-19 pandemic, I was on a video call with Kevin, a professor and higher education administrator. He shared vulnerably about the challenges of moving his courses online, providing access to students from marginalized communities who didn't have the same resources his more privileged students had, and his personal fear for his immunocompromised daughter and her desire to be as "normal" as possible.

I asked him what he needed.

"I need someone to help me carry all of these hard things. I don't need them to take them away, because no one can. I just need some help. I need to know I am not alone as I try to figure out what to do next," he mused.

"Let me rephrase my question: Who do you need with you in this season?" I asked.

He smiled and said, "You are totally right—that is the better question. I know exactly who I need to talk to. I have a holy friend who I bet is feeling the exact same way in their setting. We can carry these heavy things together."

As I proceed from topic to topic, I begin to feel lighter and less burdened because Jean is "holding" all my thoughts, feelings, and frustrations in the moment. As I feel lighter, I often gain clarity and discern solutions to some of my problems and then describe them out loud. When I am done putting things in the basket, I pause and appreciate the relief I feel because I am not carrying such a heavy load on my own. Jean will then say something like this: "This is a very heavy basket. You have a lot going on, and I am sorry you felt like you had to carry all this for so long on your own. Thank you for trusting me to hold your basket for you. What would you like to do with the basket? Do you want to talk about anything in it? Do you want to circle back to something later? I'm not going to do anything without your permission and direction, so you tell me how you want to proceed."

At that point, I usually feel calmer, more thoughtful, and clearer about a way to move forward with authenticity, intentionality, and focus. My basket may still be heavy, but because Jean held it for me while I made sense of its contents, I have a better idea of what is in it, what my priorities should be, and what my next right steps need to be. Most often, I only need her to be present and listen while I talk. Other times, I will select an item from the basket and ask for help, advice, or feedback. The choice is always mine. I also know, because Jean is my holy friend and she is invested in my flourishing, that if I mention something that is potentially harmful to me or someone else, Jean will ensure I am paying appropriate attention and taking care.

Therapists, counselors, and coaches often hold space for their clients, albeit in a transactional way, because they are paid for their services. The practice is different with holy friends because we choose to open ourselves up to mutually respectful and thoughtful critique, admonition, feedback, and advice. Our holy friends take holding space a step further because of the mutuality of the relationship, which helps us hold each other accountable to who we say we want to be and the call God has placed on our lives.

The way holy friends hold space for each other can be as different as each holy friend. Over time and through shared experiences, holy friends figure out what rhythm of conversation, feedback, advice, and accountability works for them. Often, I can tell from the tone of a holy friend's voice if they need me simply to be present while they talk, cry, or remain silent or if they are seeking affirmation, counsel, or accountability. This care is rooted in our unwavering support, our commitment to each other's flourishing, and God's unconditional love.

ACCOUNTABILITY

Byron needs his holy friends to hold him accountable for his priorities. He wants to accomplish so much in a day and regularly tries to convince himself, "If I just plan better, I can do more." While there may be some small bit of truth in his thinking, everyone gets the same twenty-four hours in a day. His thought process can lead to overscheduling and overcommitting.

Because of this pattern, Byron had to make hard choices and give up meaningful opportunities enough times that he knew he needed to change. His holy friends challenged him to clarify what gifts he wants to use to reach specific vocational goals within the next year. Now Byron can look at an invitation through a specific lens to determine if it will use his gifts and contribute to his goals. Byron's holy friends love witnessing his excitement about new opportunities. They also love him enough to ask him questions that call him back to who he says he wants to be and what God is calling him to do.

Lucia has a similar relationship rooted in accountability with her holy friends. She relies on them to help her be true to who God is calling her to be. She explains,

I need my holy friends to hold me accountable to my core questions: Who is God? Who am I? and What is God calling me to be? My holy friends and I share a sense of harmony, fierceness, and freedom that we can dare to speak truth to power if we perceive another has power. My holy friends call me on my crap, and they aren't afraid of me.

When I have my holy friends around me, I can grow. They hold me accountable when I'm angry and say, "OK, I'll hear that. I'll receive that. Now how do you want to go forward so you are godly? How do you want to go forward in a way that you're representing Christ in you, because you said that's the life you want to live? You said you want to live in a way that is beautiful and true and holy, to be a vessel of God." In my hard and messy life, holy friends are people who don't allow me to be ignorant to the deep complexities and sin that I have and will always ensnare me. We hold each other's struggles and then ask, "Now who's the person that you want to be moving forward?"

It's not easy to find such wise people. Most of my holy friends are very smart people. I want to be around them because what they offer is nurturing and life-giving to me. I pray that the Spirit is behind that and I am bringing them what they need.

Grant needs his holy friends to risk saying hard things to him to reorient him toward Christ. He remembers,

One of my best friends called me on the phone unexpectedly. I had sent him a text a few minutes before. He could tell I was having a hard time with the honors one of my former colleagues from twenty years ago was receiving. This colleague wasn't always fair to me or others. When I answered the call, he didn't say hello or bother with the pleasantries. He just said, "This is really stuck in your craw, isn't it?"

In that moment, he acknowledged my discomfort, and he pointed to Jesus Christ. In that moment, without any other words, he said, "Love this person. Forgive the past." In that moment, without any words, he asked: Are you going to follow Jesus or not?

TRAUMA

Adelina recalls the story of when Rachel was present with her in the most traumatic moments of her life. Rachel showed how priceless holy friends are when we experience trauma:

> I texted you [Rachel] early in the morning when the scandal around my father, a prominent Christian leader, became public. I asked if we could meet, and you immediately invited me to your office. I showed up and told you everything about his wrongdoings and how I was wrapped up in the trauma. I was terrified to see my parents. You listened and asked, "Do you want me to drive you to Atlanta?" Of course I wanted you to make that four-hour trip with me, but I was afraid to say it and tried to be polite and decline.
>
> You canceled your day and drove us to my hometown. You stayed with me while I gave my statement to denominational representatives, and you sat next

to me when I met with my parents. It was the hardest conversation of my life. The conversation was tense and painful.

You stayed present by my side so I never felt alone. You didn't talk much, but you pulled me aside after my dad said something really hurtful. You said, "Did you see what he did there? Did you hear what he said?" You helped me reinterpret wounding words and gave them context in his mindset of betrayal and deception. I wouldn't have been able to reframe that for a long time if you hadn't been there.

It was important to me that you witnessed the pain of that moment. You heard what was said and could remind me of what really happened if my mind started reinterpreting some of the more hurtful moments.

Something you said that was particularly powerful in that season was, "Don't let those people [the ones involved in the scandal] define church for you. They do not get to decide what the church looks like. They don't get to define that for you. You do."

Metaphorically, you created this waiting room where I could safely sit in my feelings until I figured out how to move forward in a healthy way. I don't know where I would be without you and your faithful friendship in that season. You saved my faith.

Rachel stayed quiet for most of the conversation, allowing Adelina to reflect on the painful experience. She finally spoke: "The church did you dirty. You were harmed so deeply on so many levels. I had witnessed the way you served the church tirelessly for years, and I was just praying that we could find a way to see God's redemption in such a terrible season. I know God's heart was breaking with you and for you through all of that. I also know God redeems even our biggest messes."

Rachel and Adelina's story reminds me of "sistering" in carpentry. When a piece of wood can no longer bear a certain load due to either age or damage, a new piece of wood is fastened to the original so the weight is shared by the two. Sometimes, a carpenter will "sister" a piece of wood on both sides, sharing the burden of weight among the three pieces. Holy friends who are with us in trauma "sister" our burdens so we are not breaking beneath them.

AFFIRMATION AND PROXY

Melanie, Crystal, and I have a text thread. At least twice a week, Crystal posts a Scripture text from the *Book of Common Prayer*. She usually italicizes a few lines and includes a prayer she writes for the day based on the text. I love this thread for so many reasons:

1. If I don't feel like reading all the verses, Crystal has highlighted the most important parts.
2. Sometimes the language of her prayers mirrors the language of the text—poetic and reflective. More often, there is a bite to it, a challenge in it. Sometimes the challenge is to God, and other times it is to us. Sometimes I can't tell.
3. Our continued faithfulness on the thread is not determined by how often we respond or like a post; however, Melanie and I regularly respond because Crystal almost always hits a nerve with something she writes.

4. The thread enables the three of us to walk together in a spiritual sisterhood of bravery, challenge, success, failure, beauty, ugliness, sickness, health, and everything in between.

5. This is a space where we are brutally honest with one another, sometimes saying hard truths, but mostly building one another up.

Here's a pretty typical text exchange:

Crystal: Psalm 16, *Conserva me, Domine*, BCP, p. 599

Protect me, O God, for I take refuge in you; I have said to the Lord, "You are my Lord, my good above all other."

All my delight is upon the godly that are in the land, upon those who are noble among the people.

But those who run after other gods shall have their troubles multiplied.

Their libations of blood I will not offer, nor take the names of their gods upon my lips.

O Lord, you are my portion and my cup; it is you who uphold my lot.

My boundaries enclose a pleasant land; indeed I have a goodly heritage.

I will bless the Lord who gives me counsel; my heart teaches me, night after night.

I have set the Lord always before me; because he is at my right hand I shall not fall.

My heart, therefore, is glad, and my spirit rejoices; my body also shall rest in hope.

For you will not abandon me to the grave, nor let your holy one see the Pit.

You will show me the path of life; in your presence there is fullness of joy, and in your right hand are pleasures forevermore.

C'mon Lord. You're going to come to me in the Psalms about having boundaries? About keeping out what is unhealthy and keeping in what is good?

Enclose this pleasant land. Fence in what I need, and release to the world all that is unnecessary for my well-being. God, you give me that good heritage already. I am your child. Keep my boundaries firm where they need to be. Protect me from what is unjust. Let in what needs to move and reshape me. Keep teaching me, night after night. Day by day to tend to the field of my soul with you.

Me: I am grateful you can pray this today, Crystal. . . . I can't. I read that scripture and wonder where the holy are in the land because I feel surrounded by the craptasticness of the world today. All the yuckiness. Everyone is misbehaving. The world needs a time-out.

So today I'm dialing it in on your proxy. I'm claiming redemption by my proximity to you. Thank you for praying this when I can't.

Disclaimer—this is not a cry for help or a pity-me session. It's just a statement of fact . . . and I'm two days late picking up a prescription, so I am a little chemically unbalanced. That should be fixed in a few hours. This is just life.

Melanie: That's what we do, isn't it? We hold each other's doubt and fear and anger and believe for each other. This work is hard. Love you both.

Crystal: We hold it for one another. I'm sorry friend. The world is mean and cruel, and people try to jump over the fence of our goodness all day long. We will stand watch while you heal. You will go to CVS, pick up your meds and a Snickers bar. And nail polish. I cannot promise that they won't come to try and breach your fence, but I will be standing there with you. We hold the line.

This text thread is only part of the ongoing conversations that can be picked up with the mere mention of a word or phrase: dismantling the patriarchy; fighting misogyny; relentlessly butting heads with archaic, rigged, and unjust systems; family dysfunction; books we must read; interesting people we need to know; the struggle for some sort of "flow" in life (because we are experienced enough to know that "work-life balance" doesn't exist in our lines of work); absolution for our sins; encouragement to rest; and a hundred other topics. In our texts and in our holy friendship, we are brutally honest. We egg one another on to try harder and go further—to do the hard thing or the next great thing. We call one another to consistent authenticity to the gifts and opportunities before us.

Even though we live in three cities across the East Coast, our common work as leaders in churches and Christian institutions bonds us. We hold space for one another in the present; affirm one another for the strong, faithful, and capable leaders we are and the work we do; and push one another to be all God is creating us to be in the future.

Midwifing a Vision

Holy friends orient us to what is true about our present and stir our imaginations about the future. When I was facing a crossroads in my vocation, I whined to a holy friend, "I just don't know what I want to be when I grow up."

He paused, waiting to see whether I would voice a path forward on my own. "OK," he said. "How about if we talk about who you want to be while you are growing up?"

While his response was annoying, it was also exactly what I needed from him in the moment. He took what felt like an unanswerable question—"What do I want to be when I grow up?"—and reframed it into a question I could actually answer, one that propelled me into a new and more hopeful future.

Perhaps my original question wasn't unanswerable. I could have responded with childhood dreams of being a teacher, a veterinarian, or an Olympic gymnast à la Mary Lou Retton. But it felt unanswerable. It felt complicated, final, and fraught with cascading implications. Any answer would cancel out other possibilities and set me on a path that might be irreversible.

But by reframing the question, my friend changed the focus in two significant ways. He changed the *what* to *who* and the *when* to *while*. Asking *who* makes the conversation specific to who I am and anchors it in who I will always be. I am a child of God, minister, wife, mother, sister, daughter, host, innovator, teacher, writer, and encourager. These will never change, regardless of what I "do" for a living, and I can make measurable plans to grow in each of these areas.

Asking *while* instead of *when* acknowledges that my question is ongoing. An answer doesn't appear fully formed, making the question disappear. *While* asks a question that helps me envision a future I could actually see myself living into. To reframe the musings and challenges of our holy friends is brave and creative work, especially when the questions are big. My friend could have perpetuated my frustration by saying something like, "Me neither. Let's quit our jobs, move out west, and rescue animals!" And sometimes that is exactly the response I need. Holy friends know us well enough to sense when to let us sit in our woes for a while or reorient us to the vision God has for us. Holy friends Ryan and Jace had an experience with actual visions of one of their futures.

Holy Friends Believe When We Don't

Logan was applying for the job of his dreams. Pastoring this church in this town was what he had been working toward his entire vocation. He met most of the qualifications, but he was worried about the few he didn't.

An hour before his interview with the search committee, he got an email from his holy friend Stacy. Stacy had found a copy of the church's Sunday bulletin online and made a few changes. On the cover of the bulletin, beneath the picture of the beautiful church and the congregation's motto, she superimposed, "Welcomes Logan Johnson as our seventh senior pastor." She emailed it to Logan. The image looked so real, it took him by surprise. At the end of her message, Stacy wrote, "Go into that interview and BE THEIR PASTOR. You've got this."

It was just what Logan needed to ace the interview. Stacy believed in him when he doubted himself. She gave him an actual vision of the future she knew was already his.

Ryan invested more than ten years of his vocation in growing and stabilizing a fragile Christian organization. He helped them gain more constituents and donors. He wrote grants for them. He felt good about contributing to the organization's future because he believed in its mission, vision, and values, and more importantly, he believed in his coworkers. On the really good days, he imagined himself living out his career there and really making an impact on the community.

Unbeknown to him, some of his coworkers put their desires for power and money before the good of the organization. Seemingly out of nowhere, Ryan was told his job was not included in the next year's budget. He was given two months of severance. He was gutted. How could this happen? he wondered.

Ryan had let his vocation become his identity. He was so confident in his work and his future with the organization, he'd never even dreamed of doing something else. He couldn't imagine a life without his work, and so his world became very small. Ryan fell into a deep depression.

Friends called and commiserated with him. Some tried to make connections for job interviews or new people he should meet. They sent encouraging notes and texts. Still, all Ryan could see and feel was darkness—the darkness of the betrayal of his organization, of his intuition (and arrogance) letting him think he had his life planned out, and of the death of a dream for his future.

A few days before holy week that year, one of Ryan's holy friends, Jace, reached out to him. Jace said, "I'm not really the type of person who has visions, you know that. But I was prepping for holy week services and I had a very clear vision of you. It was almost startling, so I think I need to share it with you." Ryan sheepishly laughed at the thought of his straitlaced High Church pastor friend having a vision. "OK, what was it?" he asked. Jace shared,

> You were in this really dark room—like totally dark. You had given up on ever getting out. You thought you were stuck. You couldn't see or feel a way out. But then the vision scanned up, and I saw that on the outside of each of the walls of the room, there were people, and they were praying for you, rooting for you, and anxiously waiting for you to come out. No one knew when it would happen, but we were all completely certain that it would. We knew that you are strong enough, smart enough, creative enough, and talented enough to figure out how to get out of the room. We just kind of held a vigil.

Ryan listened attentively, albeit skeptically. "You've got the darkness right. I don't know about the people. It's a nice image to think of people rooting for me. But how did it end? When and how do I get out?"

"That was it," Jace replied. "But here's what I am thinking. I saw the vision as I was preparing for holy week. See the connection? The dark room? The tomb? Not that you are Jesus or anything." They both laughed. Jace continued, "This is a really hard season for you. This loss is an actual death, of relationships and of a dream. But this is not how your story ends. It does not end in darkness. You are too talented, too gifted to stay in the dark forever. The world needs you to reemerge and let God use you for God's larger purposes. I need you, my friend; all of us, waiting on the outside, we need you."

Ryan thanked Jace for sharing his vision with him. He tried to shrug it off, but some of Jace's words stuck with him:

"This is just a season. This is not how my story ends." They became like a mantra for him as he slowly let go of some of his feelings of betrayal and anger at his former employer and grew in confidence. He began looking for a new job. He even told some interviewers, "I'm starting a new chapter. I think your organization might be a part of it."

There have been times when I wished I could bear the pain a holy friend was experiencing. Knowing we can't, sometimes the next best thing is faithfully staying alongside them, offering them grace, and reminding them of who they are as a child of God. When we can't see past our pain into the future, we need our holy friends to see it for us.

At their best, holy friends help each other envision, articulate, and apply Ephesians 3:20 to our lives: "Now to [God] who by the power at work within us is able to accomplish abundantly far more than all we can ask or imagine." Left to my own devices, I would perseverate on my past, particularly my failings, and I would be content with a smaller and less impactful version of myself. Holy friends push me to accomplish abundantly far more than I could ask or imagine for myself, my vocation, and God's work in the world. They address the gap between who I am and who God is calling me to be. Holy friends help us see the world around us not only through the eyes of others but through God's eyes so we can come alongside God's work in the world.

4

Where Do They Come From?

How Holy Friendships Emerge

Holy friends can come from as many places as there are people. Possibilities are everywhere if we are open to finding and cultivating relationships. The two primary ways I experience and observe holy friendships developing are through crucible experiences and longevity. Sometimes they develop through a combination of the two. Malcolm Gladwell's "blink" interaction is another way to recognize the potential for a holy friendship.

Holy Friendships Out of Crucibles

Certain seasons and circumstances of our lives provide the conditions for developing holy friendships. These are crucibles—places, experiences, or circumstances set apart from "regular time." They can be accidental or deliberate, and they take us out of our typical context. Think about summer camp or mission trips, when we are out of our normal environments and see the world differently as we are exposed to new people and ways of living. Think about college, a formative time when core beliefs are shaped and challenged. A crucible could also be an experience of trauma with someone, such as forming a so-called pod during the stay-at-home season of a pandemic. Crucibles can spark new growth, relationships, and habits that would not have developed without these special circumstances. The depth and intensity of crucibles provoke vulnerability and deep connection.

In the introduction, I mentioned the Vegas Girls, the five women I worked alongside when I was a chaplain in a retirement community. We were a tight-knit group because of our similar ages, families, values, interests, and work settings. We didn't know how strong we were, however, until Marcy was diagnosed with stage four colon cancer that metastasized to several major organs. For about twenty months, we stuck close together, fiercely protective of her and one another. Marcy worked in sales, so she knew everyone in the retirement community, residents and staff alike. Her spouse, Robert, worked in another office on the campus, and their two sweet boys attended the on-site child development center with all the other Vegas children. Her illness was both deeply personal to the Vegas Girls and very public in the community. She came to work as often as she could and had some good seasons we all treasured. Eventually the treatments and clinical trials ended. Time and Marcy began to quickly slip away.

The five of us banded together and cared for Marcy and her family through her death and the weeks and months that followed. We also took care of one another and our families, because as we lost Marcy, we lost a part of ourselves. The injustice and trauma of losing a young mother, wife, daughter, sister, friend, and colleague, barely into her thirties, was more than any of us could bear on our own. We carried the additional burden of having to care for a residential population and staff of almost two thousand people who dearly loved Marcy and her family.

We originally called ourselves the Vegas Girls because of the quip "What happens in Vegas stays in Vegas," alluding to the confidentiality we kept within our circle. However, in Marcy's final days, it became a shorthand for "We need to be together as soon as possible." Any one of us could send a text or an email that said, "Vegas, 3:30 Victoria's office," and everyone would show up for updates on Marcy's condition, instructions for how to disseminate information, or sometimes just to be sad, mad, and frustrated together. It was a crucible code that tied us together through a traumatic, intimate, beautiful, and brutal season. It was a season none of us wanted nor would ever choose to repeat, and yet we would not have been anywhere else.

None of us will ever forget that crucible experience. It bonded us together in a friendship unlike we have with anyone else. Some of us have moved to different jobs and locations, and yet the holy friendship remains. We can go without seeing one another for a while and pick up wherever we left off with relative ease. The crucible gave us a deep foundation for a lasting holy friendship.

Holy Friends over Time

Holy friendships can develop through the longevity of a relationship. Yes, I recognize that "longevity" is a subjective term. My father lived in the same small town for the first eighteen years of his life, and his parents never moved, so longevity for him means seventy-year friendships. Current lifestyle choices and options for remote work enable people to be more transient, thus we might move every few years. This has a direct effect on our ability to put down roots and be in physical proximity with friends. For the purposes of this book, I assume a long-lived relationship lasts at least five years.

Twenty years ago, Jonah, a Baptist pastor serving in a large southern city, met Addison, who had just moved into her first senior pastor role in a church a few streets away. Knowing they needed support and friendship beyond the two of them, they made a list of their dream team of colleagues. Who would they want to spend time with to plan sermons, discuss church issues, celebrate vocational milestones, and reflect on life together? They invited six other pastors to what came to be called Preacher Camp.

Every year, the eight pastors, and now their families, meet at a lake house for a week in the summer. Prior to arriving, the pastors divide up the year's common lectionary passages, and each prepares worship and sermon themes for their assigned texts. They spend the days listening to each one present their themes, discussing additional thoughts, and planning their next year of worship services. They spend evenings with their families, sharing food, stories, and fun.

The Legacy Class Made an Impact

Stroll the halls of a traditional Protestant church and you will likely find a hallway of classrooms marked with nameplates identifying different Sunday school classes. Some classes are named after former teachers who have passed on. Others are known by the age of the class members or how long they have been meeting. In the church of my youth, the class with the oldest members was the Legacy Class. The room was adorned with black-and-white pictures of faded faces I could barely recognize. A shelf of books displayed decades of Bible study curriculum and book groups. But it was the bulletin board of handwritten cards that always tugged at my heart. The cards were from family members thanking the Sunday school class members for their faithful friendship with their deceased loved ones. They often included a recollection of a story repeated through the years and gratitude for the flowers sent on behalf of the class. This is the tangible evidence of a lifelong holy friendship.

Each pastor leaves with much more than the notes they take. They leave with renewed energy, creativity, strength, courage, and resilience to serve the church. They leave with strengthened friendships that help them grow closer to one another and to God. The annual week together is bolstered throughout the year via a private social media page and a text thread.

Much of the chemistry and value of Preacher Camp arises from longevity—the same eight pastors gathering for twenty years. The longevity of their friendships spans marriages, divorces, raising children, burying parents, church splits, job transitions, and shifting denominational dynamics. Their sustained conversations over time enable them to pick up where they left off with ease and intimacy. Certainly, there have been crucible moments among some of the pastors in the group; however, the length of their engagement and commitment to one another provides a sacred bond for a lifetime of holy friendship.

Not surprisingly, when the pastors talk with others about their peer group, they are consistently asked whether the group receives new members. Every time, the response is, "We don't take new members. We have found what works for us. We encourage you to find or create what works for you." Group members know their chemistry is sacred, so they protect and honor it while also blessing others to find their version of a peer group that leads to lifelong holy friendships.

Holy Friendships from Longevity and Crucibles

My spouse took our kids away for spring break the year I was writing my dissertation. We were both excited about what I would accomplish while they were gone. We both needed me to finish the project, but six days of uninterrupted silence quickly became overwhelming. I began looking around the house for distractions. Pinterest became my best friend and worst enemy. I hung ridiculously trendy shelves in the mudroom and wallpapered the back wall of the pantry. The back wall. Of the pantry. On day three of the writing sprint, I had a scheduled video call to check in with a few students in my cohort about our writing progress. I proudly took the group on a phone tour of the improvements I made in the house, glowing in the "oohs" and "aahs" some of them offered.

Then Chris chimed in, "Victoria, stop it. You have been given an incredible gift of time, quiet, and dedicated space to write, and you are totally blowing it. What are you thinking? You need to sit down, get off the internet, and write."

Ouch. His words had some sting to them. The pantry was beautiful, and the shelves were totally on-trend. And he was right. My spouse and children had given me an incredibly generous gift, and I was abusing it.

I could hear Chris and absorb the sting because I trusted him. He had earned the right to say something like that to me because of the crucible we experienced together. At that time, Chris and I had known each other for only two years, but we were in a hybrid graduate program. Over the course of those two years, we endured five week-long, in-person "intensives" followed by eight weeks of online coursework. Those in-person weeks are called "intensives" for exactly the reason you think. For the waking hours we weren't in classes, we were reading, writing, talking, or complaining about classes. We got to know each other well, fast.

Chris and I have been friends for almost ten years, so we have both a crucible and longevity connecting us. We know we can count on each other for brutal honesty without having to sugarcoat our words. The way we show love for the other is by actively listening and responding with unfiltered feedback, knowing we want the best for the other.

Our holy friendship is a fairly low-maintenance one. We know enough about each other's lives that we can pick up a conversation with little need for much background information. We text at least monthly, and when we do, we text back and forth enough to have a conversation. We

FaceTime about every other month. When both of us are in the same town, which happens once or twice a year, we meet up for drinks or a meal.

We have an unspoken commitment that we are available to the other as needed. The silly stories and ridiculous GIFs we send each other are lighthearted reminders that we are thinking about and in solidarity with the other. The moment either of us sends a serious text or picks up the phone, we can fluidly move from "Hi, friend" to deep conversations with authenticity, mutual respect, and a profound desire for the other's flourishing.

Holy Friendship in a Blink

Some holy friendships are recognized in a blink, like love at first sight. There is an undeniable mutual recognition between two people. The connection feels deep, soulful, and eternal. It feels "meant to be" because we are drawn to each other with something more than or different from our heads, hearts, or bodies. It feels like forces outside of us are pulling and pushing us together.

Patrice and Nora are copastors of a church. More than twenty years separate them in age, as do experience, education, marital status, and upbringing. And yet, they share an instantly noticeable, intimate, and deep friendship rooted in mutual respect, trust, vulnerability, and love for all of God's beloved community. They remember seeing the possibility of their holy friendship in a blink.

Patrice: We were introduced in August and had our first real interaction in December. I could tell from looking at Nora that she runs deep. I

trust my "blink," as Malcolm Gladwell calls
it. From the vibes she was giving, I knew she
was good, kind, and smart. I believe the soul
is visible in the eyes, and from what I saw, I
knew I could trust her.

Nora: Our relationship went deep fast because
of the nature of the work we were doing
together. Our friendship is holy not because
of the length of it but because of the intensity of the vulnerability deposits we made
into one another over the first six months we
knew each other. This enabled us to validate
what we both assumed when we first met,
that our souls are similar. We have a soul
connection.

Patrice: Everyone assumes that women are always in
competition with one another. It is as if there
isn't enough room for all the smart women at
the leadership table. That scarcity construct
just isn't true. I loved that from the beginning, Nora wasn't intimated by me. When I
find someone who doesn't want to compete,
I'm like, "Thank God!"

Because both Patrice and Nora experienced "the blink"
when they first interacted, they were able to skip past a number of the traditional friendship "benchmarks" we often
experience when developing a friendship.

Note that Patrice and Nora said they saw the potential
for a holy friendship in a blink, not that their holy friendship happened in a blink. Still, their friendship did indeed
grow deep quickly, as Nora says, because of the "intensity

of the vulnerability deposits" they made early and quickly in their friendship.

Lizzie, a pastor with a healthy collection of holy friends, reflects in a similar way on assessing the "holiness" of holy friendships:

> When I think about our origins, about how all of this began, I didn't start any of these friendships thinking, I need holy friends. In the gift of grace, God brought these people into my life, and we journey together. Retrospectively, I can name them as holy friendships. I don't think we always have the clarity to see that in real time. I think so much of the Christian life is understood looking back, and I think the same thing is true with holy friendships. We are all journeying together, and then you realize, oh, that's really holy. That's really beautiful. So I don't think you set out to make a holy friend. It is more of being in relationship, reflecting back, recognizing it, and continuing to nurture it.
>
> When I think about it, some of our connections don't really even make sense. But at some point, we figure out something fits, and we are giving our lives to one another in a mutually life-sustaining way. Once you have experience and history together, you don't want to give that up, so you nurture it and keep it going.

Once we reflectively recognize that a relationship is a holy friendship—that it was holy and is holy—we have the knowledge and language for what we need and love about it. We are more easily able to identify the characteristics or markers of those who may be potential holy friends and intentionally invest in those relationships, knowing what is possible.

The first three times Oliver and I met, he ignored me. He never remembered that he had met me the previous times despite my attempts to have a conversation with him. I picked up on his disinterested vibes and wrote him off. The fourth time we engaged each other was in a Zoom meeting in preparation for leading a group event. He was interesting, knowledgeable, funny, and polite. I was taken aback, given our previous interactions.

At the event, he showed clear signs of wanting to get to know me: initiating conversations, asking direct questions, listening, walking next to me between events, and sitting near me when we were in the same space. I was confused. A few nights into the event, he said, "We share a number of colleagues, and our work overlaps quite a bit, so I'm surprised we haven't met before."

My looks must have betrayed my thoughts, because he went from smiling to shocked. "Are you kidding me?" I asked. "The Zoom meeting when we prepared for this event was the fourth time we have been introduced. I tried to talk to you three previous times, and each time you ignored me."

Oliver's expression became sad, and he asked, "About when were those introductions?" I gave him the dates, and he continued, "I'm so sorry. I wasn't myself in that season. I was going through a really painful divorce. It was a good day if I got out of bed, much less met other people. That wasn't me you met. That was a shell of the person I used to be. The person I am today would never ignore you. I want to get to know you. Could we start over, please?"

Oliver and I hung out together for the remainder of the week. We built the foundation for a fun, challenging (we ask each other really hard questions), intellectually stimulating, and delightful friendship. With time, ongoing conversation, and learning more about each other, our friendship turned into a holy friendship. Now we regularly collaborate on projects, consult each other for advice, and pray for each other, especially in times of crisis. And we pal around at events every chance we get.

My friendship with Oliver taught me that sometimes people are not in a good place to get to know new people or make friends. Our story reminds me that I should not presume to know what is happening in someone else's world. Oliver and I needed time to get in the right social, emotional, and intellectual headspace to begin our friendship. When I learned what he was going through years earlier and he overcame the shock of his divorce, we were both in a better place to accept each other's friendship. When we reflect on it, we have remarked to each other that we likely would have been friends from the first time we met if circumstances had been different.

There is no formula for developing holy friendship. Pastoral ministry would be easier if there were. We can't follow numbered steps or place an order for holy friends. As Lizzy says, sometimes you identify a friendship as holy only in retrospect. My holy friendship with Oliver surprised me and taught me that second, third, and fourth chances for building a friendship are sometimes worth taking. God is always working behind the scenes for our flourishing.

Holy friendships are among God's greatest gifts to us, designed to support our flourishing. Sometimes they come from those people with whom we experience a crucible or those who are by our side for the long haul. And every once in a while, we might recognize a kindred spirit in a blink. Each holy friendship has its own origin story as unique as the friends in it.

$$5$$

What Do They Look Like?

Snapshots of Holy Friendships

When I teach about holy friendship, I am regularly asked, What does a holy friendship look like in real life? How do you make time for them? How do you maintain them? What does holy friendship look like in practice? I listen to their questions, and I also hear the questions behind these questions: How do I make time for one more thing? Where does this fit between evening church meetings and the kids' swimming lessons? What is the minimum I can dedicate to this and still flourish? I know we are all strapped for time, and we are in a profession in which we are expected to sacrificially give of ourselves to others (within appropriate boundaries). In my experience, and throughout the many stories I am privileged to hear about holy friendships, once we recognize how much better we feel spending time with our holy friends and being connected to them, we can't imagine life without them, and the time organically appears out of more than necessity—out of a joyful and mutual desire for one another's flourishing.

What follows are snapshots of the lives of five healthy, successful, and flourishing leaders. I hope you will glean ideas for not only who your holy friends could be but also how maintaining these critical relationships works in our busy lives.

Soleil's Support System

Soleil knows what she needs and cultivates her own conditions for flourishing. She is a healthy, authentic, deeply spiritual, compassionate, and fierce woman. Thank God she is a pastor because the church and the world need her Christ-shaped leadership. After hearing her story, it is easy to attribute her health and flourishing to the cadre of friends she keeps around her. She knows holy friendships are critical to her thriving, thus she has cultivated multiple rings of holy friends for mutual support and care.

Soleil is a founding member of a twenty-year-old, denominationally specific clergy peer group. Years ago, she and a few other associate-level clergy worked with senior pastors who were in a successful and widely known clergy group that did not take new members (some do, some don't). Since the group they admired wasn't available to them, they began their own. Only three of the original members are still active in this intergenerational group. Some are senior pastors, others are associates. They all serve the church in some professional capacity. Through an active text stream, they share personal and professional news, offer updates to ongoing stories, ask questions, and share resources. They see one another at denominational gatherings, and they spend a week together once a year to rest, renew friendships, and take part in one another's lives. Soleil knows she could call anyone from this group for help. They share trust, intimacy, and wisdom. They all know these colleagues are accompanying one another on their vocational journeys and bear witness to their past, present, and future.

Membership in a local clergywomen's group has been another vital and intimate contributor to Soleil's ongoing health and well-being over the last five years. This dynamic group of female heads of staff includes Unitarian Universalists, Baptists, members of the United Church of Christ, Presbyterians, United Methodists, and others. They meet monthly, usually over a long, leisurely lunch in a private place away from any congregants. Anytime a new female senior pastor is hired by a church in town, they are invited to the group. No one has ever said no.

A plethora of studies attest to the unique struggles female heads of staff face in churches. Far too often, a woman is called into leadership when the church is in such decline that the leaders believe it might be time to "give a woman a try," a final Hail Mary attempt to "save it." Female pastors are regularly expected to fail. When they do, it is attributed to the leadership challenges associated with being female. When they succeed, it is viewed as a miracle or at least a lot of luck. While sexism and misogyny are among their top challenges, the list of trials is long, exhausting, and at times debilitating. Soleil explains, "We all know we need a specific kind of support. No one else can understand the work we do except one another. We are all in this together. The church needs us, and we need each other."

Soleil treasures two other groups of holy friends. One is a trio of women who are remnants of a book club that met more than twenty years ago. They knew they shared something they didn't want to lose and that they wanted to build upon. These women wish they saw more of one another, but they now live states apart. They have supported one another through a plethora of life's blessings and challenges with a lot of video calls and a WhatsApp thread. The other is a small group of interdisciplinary colleagues from graduate school. This group bonded through participating in several intensive weeks of classes, writing their dissertations, and finally graduating. They remain connected through FaceTime calls and a text thread populated by a healthy balance of genuine support and playful silliness.

Ask and You Shall Receive

Clara and I were up late at an event enjoying each other's company and talking. A younger woman joined us for a while before she said, "How do I get this, what the two of you have? I want a friendship like yours. I want the ease of conversation, the support, the laughter. You can communicate without speaking, I watched you do it earlier today. How do I get what the two of you have?"

We looked at each other and smiled in gratitude and recognition that the friendship we have is unique, rare, beautiful, and holy. We've put considerable effort into developing and nurturing our holy friendship.

While the young woman's question was flattering, she also made it clear that it was not rhetorical. She wanted to know how to cultivate the kind of holy friendship we have.

The young woman lost a few hours of sleep that night as Clara and I shared our origin story, some of our more exciting adventures, and how we maintain our friendship several states apart with busy lives and demanding jobs.

A few months later, Clara and I received a text from the young woman with a picture of her smiling cheek to cheek with another woman and the caption "#holyfriends Thanks for showing me the way."

I asked Soleil what advice she offers clergy who don't have what she has: a remarkable level of support and some really beautiful holy friendships. She admits a number of barriers keep people from creating such networks: "A lot of people are afraid to ask for what they need. They fear it might make them sound weak or needy when actually, it shows they are aware of their humanity and need for connection." Her words remind me of the African proverb "If you want to go fast, go alone. If you want to go farther, go together." None of us is meant to do ministry alone. Discerning and then asking for what we need shows we are self-aware and have assessed our context enough to know when and where we most need our holy friends.

Soleil has carefully curated groups of holy friends who root her in some of her core identities, passions, and interests: book club members from her younger years, female heads of staff, and lifelong and interdisciplinary learning colleagues. Some of these friendships have taken significantly more effort to cultivate than others, and some have formed more naturally. She has a keen eye for the value in a relationship and has the social skills to nurture certain ones into holy friendships. While some friends are closer than others, particularly in certain seasons, Soleil takes great joy in nurturing her holy friendships. She is confident she has an abundance of people she can turn to depending on the seasons of her life and vocation.

Heath's Holy Friends

Heath is a content, approachable, easygoing, funny, seemingly unflappable, low-stress Christian leader. I assume this must come from his well-honed self-awareness supported by a remarkable web of diverse holy friendships. Without giving him much definition or context from my research, I asked him to tell me about his holy friendships. He explained,

> My first thought is my spouse. We are partners and parents to our three kids, and we are copastors at the church. Our relationship began as friends in seminary. There was always a romantic connection. We love to explore, go on adventures, and we are really good at making each other laugh. I don't know if everyone is holy friends with their spouse; we are.
>
> Next, I think about this group of pastors my friend Sam introduced me to with whom I am in a peer learning group. We meet once a year for about four days. We do a book study, talk about our challenges, and encourage each other. We are intentional about supporting one another in our common work. It is a loosely structured group, and we do the things that peer groups do—the stuff that's good to do and good for you.
>
> Sam and I got to be friends in school. That was a friendship that grew deep quickly. We bonded over our vocations, families, baseball, and beer. I was gutted when he died five years ago of an aggressive cancer. I miss him a lot. I really miss what was possible with him. We would have had a lifetime of incredible friendship. I grieve the potential and possibilities that evaporated when he died.

After a moment of silence and reflection, Heath goes on to talk casually and energetically about the three friends he texts multiple times a day. "The Knuckleheads," as he calls them, met as single young adults in graduate school.

They lived in a dormitory and were on similar academic and vocational paths to being pastors. They each got married about the same time and began families within a few years of one another. Even though today they are spread throughout the country, they manage to see one another at least every other year on vacations or when passing through another's town. He describes their relationships as organic, easy, and mostly unplanned. Heath continues,

> We are really good at texting, almost hyper about it. I usually start it because I wake up in the Eastern time zone. I start with silly GIFs or a sarcastic message. Ninety percent of our texting content is nonsense. Ten percent of it is about church. We also talk and FaceTime, especially on my ten-minute walk home from church. I can FaceTime one of them and vent about what happened at work or an issue that won't go away. They don't need a backstory, so I can hop right into what is going on.
>
> I think a lot of our conversation is rooted in confession and forgiveness. We offer a safe place for one another where we can say anything without fear of judgment. We also have similar senses of humor, and so we are goofy and silly with one another. I laugh harder with them than with anyone else.
>
> We also share our sermons, and we watch recordings of each other preaching for church services. We do not offer any constructive criticism because there are plenty of voices who do that for us. Instead, we affirm and steal good stories and examples, highlight strengths, and share resources for great ideas and content.
>
> When things are hard, I find strength in knowing they are out there in the world doing similar work. Knowing they exist makes me feel less alone. Knowing

I can send a text or call them and just start talking without having to explain anything reminds me that I am seen, heard, known, valued, and connected. Even though we are goofballs most of the time, I don't know how to do life without them.

So I started out thinking that my spouse and peer learning group are my holy friends because of the intentionality and structure of those relationships. They are designed to be holy. But now that I have talked about "the Knuckleheads," those are definitely holy friendships even though much of our communication is silly and sometimes irreverent. They are my people. They are the ones I do life with, even though we are far apart. They are my pastors, friends, and brothers. In some ways, they are the least holy people I know, because we know so much about one another. We know the good, the bad, and the ugly. And we also know one another's hearts and how committed we are to our vocations, so in that way, they are the most holy of my friends.

I'm not sure who of my friends fits your definition, but these are my people.

I'm grateful Heath didn't spend too much time predetermining who his holy friends are. "My definition" is simply a place to start a conversation. Heath knows who "his people" are; he knows who he needs around him to survive and thrive in ministry and life. And he knows what kind of friendship he offers to others. That is the goal. He feels supported, validated, and like he has a community surrounding him, and he offers the same to others.

A few days after our conversation, Heath called and sheepishly confessed, "I can't believe I did this, but I left

Andy off my list when I was telling you about my holy friends. May I introduce you to him? Could we have a conversation together?"

Curious about why Heath would have forgotten to mention a holy friend and then feel the need to introduce him to me, I agreed and probed the idea. "Why do you think you left Andy off your list?" I asked.

He replied, "I've been thinking about that a lot since we talked. I think it is because we are so close. While we aren't biologically related, we are as close as brothers. Doing life with him is like breathing, I hardly think about it because we are so naturally a part of each other's lives even though we live 150 miles apart. Can we Zoom with you next time he and I are together?"

Interviewing Andy and Heath and seeing them interact was a gift of mutual joy, affirmation, and challenge. Talking about their holy friendship lit up their faces and opened a treasure chest of powerful, intimate stories. Heath began our conversation by explaining how he and Andy met.

Heath was a few months into a new pastorate when his assistant told him the Episcopal priest from down the street was waiting for him in the lobby, without an appointment. He was annoyed. Heath didn't want to talk to the priest, but there he was. Within a few weeks, they were going on walks together around the nearby university campus. Their conversations began a bit "clunky" as they pushed through small talk to figure out if they were walking with a "weirdo." Their walks turned into regular coffee meetups, which turned into lunches. Heath remembers that at some point, one of them dropped a swear word in their conversation. At that moment, they both relaxed into the friendship and began to trust each other. Heath and Andy served churches a few blocks apart for more than eight years. Their conversation flowed as naturally as their friendship.

> Andy: Being a pastor takes serious emotional labor.
> I'm always working even when I'm not
> technically working. I'm carrying around
> secondhand emotional labor that's always
> going through my head. A lot of being in
> a holy friendship for me is having a place
> where I don't have to work; I can just be. I get
> to be your friend, and I don't have to be your
> pastor. Sometimes we do pastoral things for
> one another, but most of the time, we provide
> a generous space where we take care of one
> another by not taking on each other's stuff.
> Most of the time, we are there to listen and
> remind the other to not take ourselves or our
> work so seriously.
>
> Heath: I always call you when I am losing my mind
> and feel like I am losing control. I dump all
> this stuff out, and you give me a place to leave
> it. You tell me I am not crazy and I am not the
> worst priest in the world. You tell me to give
> myself a break. You remind me that "it's just
> church," and it will still be there tomorrow.
> I know you know how it is because you are
> living it too.
>
> Andy: I am, in similar and different ways, which
> gives us enough familiarity and distance to
> be helpful to one another. For instance, I'm
> grateful that we can talk about marriage and
> how our marriages are affected by ministry.
> It's like ministry is a whole other character in

the family system. And you are able to give me a perspective I don't have, since Matt [Andy's spouse] and I don't have children. You help me see what it is like to have a family in ministry, so I can be more attentive to my staff who do.

Heath: I appreciate that you understand ministry and that our denominational polities are so different. There is no chance my complaining about something will affect any of your work in a negative way. Our work is similar enough for us to understand each other's circumstances and different enough to provide a safe distance.

I also love that there is no competition and no comparison between us. Neither one of us is switching denominations, so we will never compete against each other. There is comfort and safety in that. Competition and comparison are always just under the surface with my pastor friends in my denomination.

Andy: I understand that. I think about when I am invited to go on retreats with pastors from my denomination. These events are designed to be a relaxing time for us to be away from our churches and enjoy community with one another. But I can't relax in that environment. It is not restful for me. That is work. I'd rather you and I disappear to the farm for a few days. We can sleep, talk, not talk, and go for walks when we feel like it. You help me create the space to relax and retreat.

Looking back, Heath is grateful Andy took the initiative to stop by the office and introduce himself. He wouldn't do that for others and is still annoyed when it happens to him, but with Andy, it turned out to be an incredible gift.

One of the things unique to Heath and Andy's holy friendship is the amount of time they spent time together when they were serving in the same city. A great coffee shop and several convenient lunch spots were located between their churches. Sometimes they would meet for coffee multiple times a day. Heath explained,

> The way I saw it, I could take a break and drink stale office coffee and doom scroll on my phone for five minutes, or I could text Andy and meet him at the coffee shop. We got out of our offices, we drank good coffee, and we talked about whatever we were working on at the moment. We helped each other write sermons, solve problems, practice challenging conversations we needed to have, and work on anything else on our schedules that day. I never felt like I was doing ministry alone because even though we were in different contexts, we were doing ministry and life together.

I asked them if they were ever concerned someone might question how they were spending their time if they were together so often.

Heath: Never. I've been doing this long enough, I am confident in the kind of pastor I am. I set my schedule. I get my work done. If I choose to do some of my work in a coffee shop with another pastor, it is my choice. And having coffee with Andy makes me a better pastor,

spouse, father, and friend. When we are
together, we hold space for each other to
work things out that might otherwise unnec-
essarily spiral in our heads if we were alone.
We are better together than we are apart. It is
just the way we do ministry.

Andy and Heath's conversation volleyed back and
forth with natural ease, attentiveness, wit, and healthy
snark. Their love for their churches, vocations, families,
and each other was evident through each story and memory shared. Heath closed the conversation with a lovely
image of his holy friendship with Andy:

Heath: When I think about you, I think about the
Good Samaritan. Everything the Samaritan
did for the man on the side of the road, you
have done for me and my family. You have
literally nursed my wounds when I recovered
from surgery. You financially supported us
when we needed it. You and Matt feed me
amazing food, and you've given me generous places to stay over and over again. And
when I have been at my worst, you stuck
with me until I was OK on my own again.
You show up for me in undeserved and
unconditional ways.

After spending time with Heath and Andy and witnessing the ease and bond between them, I better understood
why Heath forgot to include Andy in his original reflections on holy friendship. Their souls are connected. Their
lives, ministries, and families became intertwined when

they worked in proximity to each other, and the connection remains, albeit in a different form now that they are separated. Their holy friendship is so much a part of who they are and how they function in the world, it can appear as if it happens without effort. The time and intentionality they put into their relationship for the many years when they saw each other multiple times a day built a solid foundation on which they now rely. Their holy friendship has the strength and resilience to flourish through texts, calls, and visits a few times a year.

You Are Too Important to Me

Ken knows his holy friends are "different" in this way: "I have other friends who I just can't go to very serious places with, because if we got to a certain level of disagreement, I don't think the relationship would make it. I think that is what sets holy friendship apart. We have conflicts and we disagree all the time, but we don't let it endanger our friendship. Our commitment to each other forces us to return to hard conversations until we figure them out. My holy friends are too important to me to not figure our stuff out."

Hannah and Evangeline:
All in the Family

Some people immediately think of family members when they think of their holy friends. Hannah and Evangeline, biological sisters who also see themselves as holy friends, opened my eyes to new ways of being family that are as hopeful as they are beautiful. Hannah is two years older than Evangeline. They explained:

Hannah: I have four siblings, but I have a holy friendship only with Evangeline. I think we have
made a different kind of commitment to one
another to intentionally nurture our friendship above and beyond our relationship as
sisters.

Evangeline: We've had to work hard together to break
through some family systems to enable us
to be honest with one another in ways we
wouldn't have without our commitment to
being friends.

Hannah: Being holy friends and sisters can be a
challenge sometimes because we have family
history and a built-in future. We don't have a
choice in knowing what we know about the
other. You literally can't get rid of me.

Evangeline: I think our holy friendship happens because
we have intentionally built this friendship.
You and I experience joy, pain, and everything in between in a deeper way because our
relationship is more layered, more complex.
We choose to cherish our relationship as
sisters and take it a step further as we experience the real stuff of life as holy friends.

Hannah: We figured out when we were young adults,
early in our marriages and starting families,
that we needed and wanted something more,
different, richer than what we had as sisters. Some of it was intuition for the kind of
support we knew we needed to live the lives

we wanted. And some of it is just that I love you and you're everything I would want in a friend. I'm just so lucky we are both.

Evangeline: Within our family system, the status quo is really important. We all work hard to keep each other happy and in our designated roles. Our holy friendship pushes us to see each other in an alternate story line—in God's story and our family story. Within God's story, we push each other differently. We challenge and affirm and hold each other accountable. I know I don't do that with our other siblings because I think I'd be kicked out of Thanksgiving dinner.

Hannah: Our family appreciates politeness. We are not polite in our holy friendship because we don't need to be. We cut through the fluff to what is real, raw, and authentic.

I think our relationship really grew from sisters to holy friends who are also sisters when our brother Jack died. That changed all of us. It crumbled all the rules, and nothing made sense anymore.

Evangeline: And you and I were experiencing other personal trauma at the same time that drew us together. I remember when we were in the middle of Jack's death, and I told you about a mistake I had made that I thought was the worst thing I had ever done. Here I was pouring my heart out to you in tears, and you laughed! You laughed and said, "Well thank God you are human. I have always wondered." In that moment, I remember feeling full acceptance from you, and I felt safe, even in all the pain. That was when I knew you would love me no matter what, like a sister and a friend. You loved me in my greatest failure.

Hannah: There is safety in our relationship that I don't have with anyone else. I can tell you anything and you won't judge me, belittle me, or make me feel like less of a person. You won't condone everything I do, but you accept and love who I am. You are safe to me, with me, for me. I feel your love and support no matter what I bring to you, even when I think I am the worst person on the face of the earth.

Do you remember when I called you when Chad [Hannah's ex-husband] left? You packed up your four children in your minivan and drove halfway across the country to be with me and my kids. Who does that? Those big moments and all the little moments along the way have built something between us that our other siblings can never understand, even if they wanted to. And we have tried including them in our more intimate connections multiple times throughout the years, individually and together. They seem content keeping our relationships the way they have always been—distant.

Evangeline: It is important to me that a lot of our holy friendship is rooted in us having fun together. Even though we live eight hours apart, we love doing life together by meeting up whenever we can, talking often, and texting every day. You are one of my favorite people.

Hannah: I feel the same. I love watching the person you are growing into right now. You are clearly leaning into your gifts and strengths that are affecting every area of your life. It is amazing watching you blossom into this powerhouse of a woman God is designing you to be.

Evangeline: That is something that has come out of our friendship that was never accessible in our sisterhood: we are now one another's biggest cheerleaders. The competition is gone. We only want the very best for each other. I love that about us.

Knowing these two women and watching their friendship and sisterhood deepen through career changes, divorces, and relationships with young adult children is a beautiful gift. At times, I am jealous of what they have because I never had a biological or familial sister. But I am never jealous for long because they kindly count me as one of their chosen sisters. It is what holy friends do for each other.

When folks ask what holy friendships look like in practice, my answers vary because they look different for everyone. Notice that in Soleil and Heath's circles, many of their holy friends are in ministry. They also have friends in dramatically different lines of work. Conversations with friends who are different from us can provide a quick and easy escape from the challenges of ministry in addition to stretching our imagination with new ideas and ways of seeing the world. Diversity among our holy friends helps us grow in empathy, curiosity, and self-awareness and more fully appreciate and participate in one another's stories in seasons of flourishing and challenge.

Sometimes We Need
Other Holy Friends

I would be remiss if I weren't honest about the challenge that sometimes comes with having holy friends. My holy friendship with Diana was tested when she went through a very public and painful trauma. She was betrayed by someone she believed was a holy friend. It was personally and professionally devastating to her, and it played itself out in the media in a way that misrepresented her in every possible way. A number of people she thought were friends disappeared when she was no longer the shiny, powerful, connected version of herself.

It was hard to be a holy friend with Diana in that season. I never once dreamed of not being beside her, and yet it was difficult. A very small group of friends and family took turns being her support, because no one person could bear the weight of walking with her in such hateful and evil darkness.

I figured out quickly that for me to support her in the way she needed, I needed to have my holy friends supporting me. I connected regularly with two dear friends who were invaluable to me in that season. They had a basic idea of what was happening and knew I was at the center of Diana's support. I could call and be angry, frustrated, sad, overwhelmed, and exhausted. They held space for me. They couldn't do anything except listen to me. I would care for Diana until I couldn't anymore. I would call them and cathartically expel all the feelings that built up inside me—some of my own stuff and some secondhand trauma from being so close to Diana. They would encourage and affirm me and send me back into the arena ready to care for her again. I couldn't have survived that season without them. To this day, Diana knows I had others supporting me so I could support her. She doesn't know who they are and doesn't need to know. She is grateful.

My family had front-row seats to learn what a holy friendship in crisis looks like. My spouse kept our household moving when I would visit Diana for a few days at a time. He got to see me love someone deeply through my words and actions. My children came to love her and understand why I was sad, stressed, or angry during those months. They watched a cadre of incredibly strong, creative, and resourceful women and one man surround her in her weakest moments and nurse her back to a level of health she could sustain on her own. My kids saw me as more than a mom, wife, daughter, or minister. They saw me as a holy friend.

Because Diana and I have big personalities and stubborn righteous streaks, sometimes our relationship can be tumultuous and exhausting. And yet, I cannot imagine my life without her. Diana and I were close before she suffered through her traumatic season. While we were in the thick of it, she had very little to contribute to our friendship. She needed my support. Now that she is on the other side and thriving in creative new expressions of her vocation, our holy friendship has returned to equilibrium but with a deeper connection and a reinforced conviction that we are meant to do life together, no matter how hard it gets. Her soul is connected to mine because together, the way we live, love, and work matters and makes a difference in the world. We are stronger together than we could ever be apart.

We need to know what kind of support we need so we can support others. Sometimes a loved one faces a challenge that is so painful, the secondhand trauma of the caregivers requires a specific kind of attention. Asking for this support is a sign of strength and self-awareness. It is also a sign of resilience for our friendships because we know what we need to sustain ourselves to be available to our holy friends in crisis. It is what we do to stay in relationship with the ones we love the most, knowing that seasons change. We trust that at some point, the crisis threshold in our friendship will wane and we will be able to figure out a new normal having survived together, because there is no place else we could imagine being.

The stories in this chapter are mostly about leaders who have multiple holy friends. We remember, though, that having more holy friendships does not lead to greater flourishing. David has been a pastor for more than thirty years, and he has one holy friend. David and Mindy have walked alongside each other in ministry for the past thirteen years. Mindy has several holy friends because her personality is such that she needs and wants to give and receive that level of friendship. David, on the other hand, is content with one holy friend, and he is flourishing in his church. Whether your personality and place in life allow you to have one or multiple holy friendships, of utmost importance for your personal and professional flourishing is that you have at least one person with whom you share a holy friendship.

6

Should My Friends Be Different from Me?

Navigating Difference and Privilege

I thought I was going to get fired at the beginning of Advent the first year I served as a chaplain in a retirement community. The majority of the residents in the community were Presbyterians and Episcopalians, so as a Baptist, I was learning a lot about their more "High Church" traditions around liturgy and worship.

Part of my job was to place twenty-two manger scenes throughout the campus. A few days after I completed the task, I walked by one of the crèches and noticed baby Jesus was missing. Confused, I checked another crèche in a different area of campus and found baby Jesus and the wise men were gone. Alarmed, I retraced my steps and discovered that in all twenty-two manger scenes, baby Jesus was missing, and in about half of them, the wise men, and often the camels, were also gone.

Who would do such a thing? What kind of person steals figures from manger scenes, and in particular Jesus?

I sheepishly told my supervisor what had happened and braced for the worst. He laughed. A lot. "Don't worry about it," he said. "It's so normal to me now, I don't put Jesus or the wise men out in Advent either."

"What are you talking about? It is not a manger scene without those figurines! Jesus is the whole point of the manger scene!" I said exasperated.

He laughed even more, sensing my conviction. "A lot of our residents come from church traditions in which you don't put Jesus in the manger until Christmas Day, and then the wise men and camels do not arrive until Epiphany. No one stole baby Jesus."

My looks betrayed me, and he continued, "I can see you are bothered by this. It has nothing to do with you. It is the way others celebrate Advent. I promise the people who 'took' those figures were probably just as bothered to find them *in* the manger scenes as you are finding them *missing*." He paused. "Wait it out, and I am certain that Jesus will make his arrival on Christmas Day, all twenty-two of him."

That was the longest Advent season of my life. But sure enough, baby Jesus made his grand entrance to all the mangers on Christmas Day. The wise men, their gifts, and their camels arrived on Epiphany.

Every Advent since then, when I set up manger scenes around my home, baby Jesus and the wise men are present in all of them except one. I pick a different one each year and keep Jesus and the wise men tucked away until their timed arrivals. Their absence reminds me that my way of celebrating Advent, Christmas, and everything else about my faith is one expression of many possible ways to experience God's love. Different ways of celebrating our faith, being a good neighbor, and loving God help us appreciate the beautiful diversity of God's creation and the abundant paths to beloved community.

While differences in how we display our manger scenes are not significant (although try telling that to the devout Episcopalians who stole baby Jesus), it never ceases to amaze me how quickly people allow small differences of opinion to evolve into enormous issues. Many of us say we want to embrace difference and diversity, and yet when it comes time to change "the way we have always done things," our convictions do not feel so . . . convincing.

We know sharing life with others who see the world differently from the way we do makes us more empathetic, compassionate, and understanding humans. When you reflect on your friendship map, though, how much diversity do you see with regard to race? Ethnicity? Gender? Socioeconomic background? Political affiliation? Education? Faith? Does your friendship map look fairly homogenous, or does it represent the diversity of God's beloved community? We are naturally drawn to people who look, think, behave, believe, and live like we do. This innate desire is rooted in our animal instinct to survive. We believe we are safer with people "like us."

Unfortunately, when we do not experience other ways of thinking, believing, and living, we risk overlooking some of the most interesting aspects of God's abundantly diverse creation. When we acknowledge the lack of diversity in our friendships, however, we are often quick to blame our contexts. We ignore the fact that in our basic human instinct to survive, we are naturally drawn to people who are more like ourselves. We follow this instinct in choosing where to live, where to go to church, where to send our children to school, and where to shop. And yet, diversity makes communities stronger, more resilient, and more likely to thrive. Diversity within our holy friendships enables us to live and love in more Christlike ways.

When I was articulating my definition of holy friendships—mutual and sacred relationships deeply formed in God's love—the word *mutual* was the last term I added to the definition because it was the most challenging to get right. I briefly considered *equal*, but equality among two people is rare. One of the pair typically has more power, influence, or privilege in some area of their friendship. This is especially true within holy friendships among persons who are different and diverse. The more ways friends are different, the more unequal their power may be both as individuals and within their larger contexts. And sometimes inequality is attributed not to "more" or "less" difference and/or power but to the particular ways we are different from one another. Because of our society's historically oppressive social, political, and economic structures, friends' power dynamics and access to privilege are rarely equal. Thus, in my definition, I chose *mutual* because belonging to one another as God's beloved children transcends (but does not ignore) differences. Holy friends intentionally belong to one another, and they acknowledge their intimate and holy connection to one another and the world, differences and all.

While our society is making progress (albeit slowly) in addressing systemic injustices and generational inequalities among minoritized populations, pastors and Christian leaders have a responsibility to share their resources and access to privilege with others. The Gospel of Luke reminds us, "From everyone to whom much has been given, much will be required, and from the one to whom much has been entrusted, even more will be demanded" (Luke 12:48). Within the sacredness of our holy friendships, we recognize and validate the differences among our friends, treasuring the complexity while also working to dismantle the systems that perpetuate discrimination, prejudices, and unequal access to resources.

As I began thinking about who to interview for this book, Carlyle and Rose were at the top of my list. Carlyle pastors "Vinci Community Church," an outdoor church plant for the housing insecure population of her community, and Rose pastors "the Fora," a womanist church started a few towns away. I had been hearing Carlyle talk for years about her friendship with Rose. Through Carlyle's stories but without having met Rose, I coveted their friendship. I am in awe of their vulnerable and authentic conversations about race, privilege, and identity, among many other topics. They shared generously about race and privilege at the outset of our conversation, when I asked each of them what they bring to and receive from their friendship. They tell their story much better than I ever could:

Carlyle: A while back, Rose invited me to be on her podcast, and we talked about friendship between Black women and white women. We talked through our experience about complications that arise, most of the time for reasons out of our control. Things get out of balance because of the difference in our privilege. I think we work hard to push through the complications to maintain this core of mutuality and love that we've had for so long. I think that's been the work of the Spirit in each of us and between us both.

I'm grateful for the honest experiential wisdom you bring to our friendship. You keep me from making some really big mistakes. When I was planting Vinci Community

Church, I called you and said, "I'm going to leave my job, and I'm going to plant an outdoor multiracial church, and we're going to embody racial diversity. What do you think?" And you said, "But you're white." And I said, "I know." And you said, "Who are you going work with?" And I said, "I don't have anybody; it's just me." And you said, "Uh, you can't do that. You can't just decide that." If anyone else had said that to me, I would have felt shame. But you didn't shame me. You told me how not to do it and then very patiently explained why in a way I could understand.

Rose: You have to have some credibility with Black people, with Hispanics, or any minority group in order for them to trust you, and I didn't see any of that in your world.

Carlyle: My ideas don't come from a bad place. I am trying to do good, and you see that and give me a generous space to figure out where I am being clumsy and need to rethink things.

I'm so grateful that you don't "call me out" when I voice an off-the-wall notion. I feel like rather than calling me out for my clunky ideas, you call me in. You call me nearer to you, to your perspective, or to an insight that I didn't have before. And there is never any shame.

Rose: These kinds of friendships are so important between Black women and white women. But the friends have to be able to be honest. As a Black woman, I have insights and perspectives that you don't and can't have, and vice versa. It's important to help one another see things on a deeper level, in ways that we hadn't imagined.

Carlyle: We have talked about how I bring privilege to this relationship that I want to share with you. Vinci Community Church is five years old, and your church, the Fora, is three years old. Vinci Community was planted in part because I was ready to leverage a bunch of privilege that I had built up in our denomination. A lot of that is about whiteness, and a lot is about playing the political games within the denomination. I called in a number of favors to collect a "yes" in support of my idea. That yes meant money and a platform from which I could ask for more money.

The Fora was not launched from privilege. By the time you were launching, there wasn't as much money and not as many platforms from which to ask for it.

Because I knew the Fora was at a disadvantage, I wondered, How do I leverage not just dollars and cents but some of the privilege of those same connections for this project that I believe in and you, my sister church planter, who I love? How I do figure out how much heat I can take for telling people in our region or denomination that if they let the Fora die for lack of funds, it is shame on us? I can say that, and you can't.

Rose: Maybe our gift to each other is insight. By virtue of who you are, your privilege, and your

boldness, Carlyle, you offer me insights into
the currencies of our denomination. You help
me see what is available and help me figure out
how to leverage it. You know things I don't
know. And I share insights with you in what
I know through my work and situation in life.

Carlyle: Remember when you were starting the Fora,
and you described the plan to me? You said
there were going to be three women who
would take turns preaching—three womanist
collaborators because, you said, "this is the
womanist way." And I said, "I'm sure those
other two women are fine. But my interest
is you, and you don't have enough money
for the three of you to do this work. You are
going to have to keep doing side gigs and look
for health insurance. I'm worried about you,
and I think you need to ditch them and do
this on your own."

Rose: I didn't say anything in the moment, but I
was thinking, "Carlyle, I know you love me.
But you don't have any of this right." So I
waited a few months and brought the topic
up again.

Carlyle: You told me that feminism wants to kick
open the door and get in the room with the
men. What womanism wants is to tear down
all the walls, so there's no more room, so the
room doesn't exist. And when you said that,
I thought, "I got it all wrong. Now I can see
what you are doing. Now I get it." Watching
you and the other pastors has helped me
be a better collaborator with my staff. For

instance, I watch how you give up the pulpit. In typical white churches, you don't give up the pulpit; the pulpit is where your power is.

Rose: That's exactly what we are trying to do. We are trying to deconstruct the power and leverage it so everyone feels empowered. We have more collective power when we give it away.

Carlyle: That really threw me off. You relinquish power and [do] not grasp on to it. I think about Philippians 2:5–7, "Have this mind among yourselves, which is yours in Christ Jesus, who, though he was in the form of God, did not count equality with God a thing to be grasped, but emptied himself." How bold is it that as a Black woman, you are not grasping but divesting? I just didn't understand.

Rose: It is the way of womanism to release and share. That is where the real power is, and that is gospel. And I think it goes along with the relationship between our churches. We don't fall into the old model of competition. There's no sense in that. If one of us gets better, we all get better.

Carlyle: For me, our friendship is important for many reasons, and in particular because of the effect our relationship has on our churches. We both keep telling our congregations that we are not alone in this gospel work. We have friends at the Fora or at Vinci Community who are doing this very hard work in a way and in a place that we can't. And it's important that we rise together.

It has taken several years, countless hard conversations, and a handful of crucible experiences for Rose and Carlyle to build the foundation of trust and candor they share in their holy friendship. Their honesty and self-awareness about what they each bring to their friendship are examples of the mutuality I seek to embody in all my friendships. They boldly address their differences and courageously seek to use their access to build up each other's ministries according to their expertise, experience, and privilege. They are clear that not only do they (and their churches) need each other; they embrace their differences to strengthen each other.

Rose and Carlyle's holy friendship helps them be better humans, pastoral leaders, neighbors, and members of their community. Their churches are healthy and thriving in ways unique to their contexts, thanks in part because they have healthy leaders. Rose and Carlyle know they need each other's friendship, candor, wisdom, support, love, and privilege in order to be the brave and bold leaders God calls them to be.

Sameness Does Not Equal Success

Jayden thought he was a healthy leader. He was in a peer group. He participated in a few affinity community clubs. He stayed in touch with some friends from college. And he had a trusted handful of holy friends with whom he shared loyal, vulnerable, and tight-knit relationships.

Jayden is the kind of friend who remembers birthdays and other special occasions. He takes his friends to lunch when he senses they need to talk. He enjoys several text threads among his groups of friends. They chat about everything from sports to their families to current events.

There Is Room for More

Cynthia wondered if she was "cheating" on her holy friend Ash when she sought to deepen a friendship with someone much different from Ash. She and Ash had been inseparable since childhood, and they knew everything about each other. Cynthia began to sense she needed a friend with whom she didn't have as much history, someone who could give her a perspective different from the one she could predict Ash would give her.

Ash noticed Cynthia was behaving oddly and asked her what was going on. Cynthia told them about her growing friendship with Simon. Ash was touched Cynthia was worried about them. They took it as a sign of love and commitment to their lifelong friendship. Ash also blessed Cynthia's budding friendship with Simon. Ash said, "As we age, we are each becoming more complex humans. We may have been the perfect friends growing up, meeting all of each other's needs. But we are beyond that. I bet your friendship with Simon will strengthen, rather than weaken, our friendship. Your heart is so big, you always have room for more friends. And if the time is ever right, I'd love to meet Simon. He must be pretty great if he gets to be your friend."

When Jayden became frustrated by a particular political event, he turned to his friends to rant with them. They all agreed with him and in some ways even exacerbated his irritation. After a few days of exchanging texts, calls, and water cooler conversations, Jayden made an off-handed comment to a colleague he didn't know very well. The colleague responded, "Wow. I'm surprised to hear you say that so confidently. You know not everyone thinks the same way you do about that."

Jayden flushed and recognized what he had done. He'd created a circle of friends who all shared basically the same views, backgrounds, experiences, education, and outlook on life. He was living in an echo chamber that reinforced his own thoughts, so he rarely heard any contradicting points of view. His friends were all good people. They went to church and tried to live Christlike lives. He thought his social circles contributed to his health as a leader, which they did, in many ways. However, they were also perpetuating small-mindedness and toxic thinking.

He returned to the colleague who had so bravely confronted him and thanked him. Jayden asked if he would introduce him to some of the people his colleague referenced who think differently. Jayden also began seeking out and cultivating friendships with people from varying backgrounds, experiences, places, and beliefs. Jayden realized to be the best version of himself and fully live into who God is creating him to be, he needs to surround himself with a better representation of God's diverse, beloved community.

It Isn't Easy

One of the things I love about Rose and Carlyle's friendship is their adamant refusal to accept the status quo. They call out the systemic injustices in front of them and work together to dismantle them in the long term and share privilege in the short term. They don't shy away from hard conversations about what is different between them; rather, they lean into their differences and find ways to use them as opportunities to benefit each other and their churches.

Cultivating and nurturing a relationship like Rose and Carlyle's requires an "extra dose" of vulnerability, time, and trust. Those from majority groups need to avoid placing pressure on those from minority groups to help them find new and better ways to be in relationships that provide for mutual flourishing. "Majority-Culture Savior Syndrome" can arise in even the most well-intentioned and self-aware leaders, as can defensiveness and inadvertent appropriation. Open-mindedness, curiosity, patience, humility, and empathy go a long way in nurturing any relationship but particularly those across cultural divides. A sense of humor helps too because no one is perfect. Everyone makes assumptions and mistakes. Holy friends offer us grace as we come alongside one another and see the world through each other's eyes, which places us one step closer to seeing with God's expansive and diverse vision.

7

Do These Relationships Count?

What Holy Friendships Are Not

One way to define something as complex and nuanced as holy friendships is to clarify what they are not. In order to be involved and invested in one another's lives the way holy friends are, the relationship cannot be transactional or hierarchical. That is, the friends must have equal power in the relationship (recognizing that in certain seasons, one friend might be in greater need and therefore have less power than the other). For this reason, holy friends are different from pastors, mentors, spiritual directors, therapists, coaches, and others in similar professional listening roles. The people who fulfill these roles are often holy people in our lives, and some of them may be our friends. Nonetheless, they do not take the place of holy friends.

Typically pastors, therapists, spiritual directors, coaches, and mentors receive specialized education and training to do their work. Although our relationships with people in such roles are in some ways similar to holy friendships, the power imbalance in the relationship typically inhibits authentic mutuality and two-way vulnerability. Two aspects of such relationships are important. First, if someone is trained to listen to you and help you solve problems, the relationship is not mutual. Second, if someone is paid to listen to you, the relationship is not mutual. When we yield to the expertise of a paid professional to whom we have come for help, no matter how much we enjoy each other's company, there is a power differential preventing mutuality.

When I map my relationships (chapter 2), I put these significant yet transactional connections in an adjacent category I call "transcendents." My pastor, coach, mentors, therapist, and spiritual director are present on my map but not included in my holy friendship circles. They nurture and sustain my health and well-being. They are important enough to have on the map because they contribute to my flourishing, but they do not fit the criteria of holy friends.

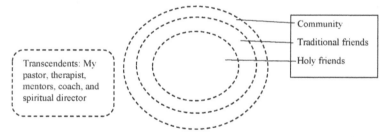

Figure 7.1 My friendship map with transcendents

Holy Friends Are Different from Pastors

I was ordained on a beautiful April afternoon in the historic Williamsburg Baptist Church in Virginia. According to my denomination's tradition, there was a time in the service in which I knelt on a padded kneeler, and everyone present (who felt so called) "laid hands" on me. Some held my hands, others put their hands on my head, others squeezed my shoulders, and still others knelt in front of me so I could see their faces as they spoke. They offered affirmations, prayers, blessings, and well-wishes for my ministry. It was powerful and memorable. The service also included a charge to the candidate (advice in the form of a homily to me) and a charge to the congregation (advice in the form of a homily to the church I would serve). Clergy and academics in dark heavy robes processed up and down the center aisle. It was a lovely service of worship, ordination, and a bit of mystery.

The next week, a youth who had been at the ordination asked me, "When did it actually happen? Because I think I missed it. When in the service did you go from being Victoria to Reverend Victoria or Pastor Victoria, or what do we call you now? The bulletin didn't say, so I think I missed the moment." Her question is a good one. I tried to explain the yearlong ordination process of meetings, writing papers, more meetings, a congregational gathering in which anyone could ask me anything they wanted about anything, and finally the ordination service. But really, her question was, "When did you change? When did you become something different?"

Pastors are "something different." The point of my ordination service was to "set me apart" from the rest of the congregation as someone "called" into vocational ministry. The nature of pastors being "something different" sets up power differentials between pastoral leaders and congregants. The difference in power, while interpreted in varying ways across denominations and faith traditions, muddies the waters for relationships rooted in mutual vulnerability.

Many parishioners love and want to be friends with their pastors. This sentiment helps foster healthy pastors who lead healthy congregations. Parishioners often assume a level of intimacy and shared life between them and their pastor, not recognizing that the transactional and hierarchical nature of these relationships prevents them from being truly mutual.

Congregants may feel a sense of mutuality because many pastors share stories about their life and family in their sermons and teaching, and pastors are often present at significant moments in a family's life such as baptisms, weddings, surgeries, deaths, and traumas. This sharing of stories and collective experiences can give the illusion of a growing intimacy (similar to what can happen on social media) as parishioners learn more about a pastor's life. But pastors often participate in a parishioner's life because they are fulfilling a leadership role for the congregation or a ritual role related to members' faith commitments.

Pastors cannot be holy friends with their congregants. Certainly, many pastors have social friendships with parishioners that are healthy platforms for contributing to beloved community. But a pastor's holy friends must be from outside their congregation. I highly recommend pastors cultivate holy friendships with other pastors—inside or outside your denomination, whichever feels more comfortable to you—and/or with other Christian leaders. Friends who identify with the opportunities and challenges of ministry contribute to our joy and decrease our burdens.

One pastor I interviewed mused about whether a pastor and congregant can be holy friends. "There's just such great risk involved," she said. If the holy friendship sours, the congregant could be left without a pastor. She said there is plenty of opportunity for friendships and sharing of life between a pastor and parishioner, but keeping certain boundaries is a matter of respect for each other's well-being.

Holy Friends Are Different
from Mentors

Mentor-protégé relationships are personal and yet intentionally unbalanced in power, knowledge, skills, and other possible traits. Much like a holy friend, a seasoned and accomplished mentor senses promise and mutually shared values within a protégé. A mentor invests in their protégé and strives to help them succeed. While the mentor and protégé might desire each other's flourishing, there is a clear hierarchy in the relationship as the mentor challenges their protégé to stretch themselves, to grow and learn.

Another way mentors are different from holy friends is that while the protégé opens themselves up to the influence and formation of the mentor, the mentor is not necessarily expected to reciprocate the vulnerability. However, in the best mentor-protégé relationships, the mentor encourages calculated risk-taking and helps the protégé ask questions they aren't asking yet, and they both help each other see the world differently. Once the protégé has learned enough from their mentor, over time, some mentor-protégé relationships, much like student-teacher relationships, can balance out and become robust peer friendships among equals.

Holy Friends Are Different
from Listening Professionals

Spiritual directors, life coaches, therapists, and counselors are important, valuable listening professionals. A relationship between them and their client is intentionally unbalanced. They are paid for their skills: walking alongside their clients; providing support, guidance, and reflection; and practicing holy listening. Some of them help their clients pay attention to how God is working in their lives and respond in faithful ways. A client can tell their listening professional things they wouldn't share with anyone else, even a holy friend. Listening professionals hold space for their clients, listen deeply, and hold clients accountable for growth, which are all things holy friends do for each other. However, the transactional nature of a listening professional's relationship with a client keeps it intentionally unbalanced.

These relationships come with highly regulated boundaries that prevent listening professionals from becoming involved in the everyday lives of their clients. While the work a listening professional and client do together often yields a sense of familiarity, the relationship is still one-way.

I've had a life coach for nineteen years. He's worked with me through two maternity leaves, two job changes, three moves, and a terminal degree program. He knows things about me no one else knows. He is retired clergy, and so his life's work—and in particular, his work with me—is rooted in his Christian vocation. He holds my past, present, and future together and helps me see God at work in ways I could not see on my own.

My relationship with my coach is one of the most intimate relationships I have. It could easily be mistaken for a holy friendship because it is a set-apart relationship like none other I have. I care deeply about his well-being and flourishing, and we share vulnerably with each other. Something holy happens when we talk. The space always feels sacred, blessed. And yet, it is a contractual one. I pay him to coach me. I pay him to ask me the hard questions a holy friend might not think to ask.

That I pay someone for what I just referred to as intimacy might sound odd. I pay him to remain in conversation with me as I struggle through challenging questions, seek to make better-informed and well-thought-through decisions, and grow toward my goals. Our relationship is different from a holy friendship because he has been trained to ask specific kinds of questions to help me get outside my head and out of my own way.

In my experience, and in those of the healthiest people I know, pastors and Christian leaders should pay professionals to meet whatever needs they have for coaching, therapy, spiritual direction, or any other listening-related services. We need to be clear about expectations and boundaries in all our relationships. We also can't expect our holy friends to bear all of our burdens with us.

Deacon is a verbal processor. He needs to talk through all the potential scenarios of a situation—the opportunities, challenges, obstacles, people involved, timing, and return on investment—before he makes a decision about anything. You name it, Deacon wants to talk about it. He's an outgoing, extroverted, and visionary leader. He has a thousand ideas before breakfast. Deacon shows up as a big personality with a lot of energy that can be overwhelming and exhausting to some of his friends.

Heather is Deacon's favorite conversation partner. They both think fast and enjoy processing the details of their ideas. They have similar backgrounds and education, so their faith has been formed in ways that make conversation easy. She also loves closure—to wrap up conversations so she can confidently move on to whatever is next. Deacon has no need for closure in a conversation, however, and will bring an idea up multiple times over the course of a discussion.

Because Heather loves Deacon and doesn't want to stifle his energy or creativity, she has developed a way for both of them to get what they need in their conversations. Heather will listen to Deacon bring up an idea five times. If at that point Heather believes she has nothing further to contribute to Deacon's idea, she will say, "Have you talked to your spiritual director/therapist/coach/mentor/ whoever the right person is for this idea? I bet they will be able to help you make some progress that I'm just not seeing." Deacon has caught on to Heather's question and her need for closure. He never wants to bore or overwhelm Heather, and he is grateful for her redirection to those who could be helpful in ways she can't.

Sometimes I look at my circles of support and marvel at the number of people I need to be physically, emotionally, and spiritually healthy and (somewhat) balanced. I'm always incredibly grateful for the access I have to them. I need a pastor, a spiritual director, a therapist, a coach, and mentors to help guide, nudge, push, and sometimes pull me into the next iteration of who God is calling me to be. Often, I need my holy friends nearby so I can complain about how hard all of those people are making me work. Every member of my paid professional support team wants me to succeed and flourish, much like holy friends do. But they cannot take the place of holy friends. For the sake of your health and flourishing, and all those you serve alongside, I encourage you to secure a varied and diverse lineup of listening professionals alongside your holy friends for your health and well-being. Because healthy pastors lead healthy congregations.

8

What Will They Cost Me?

Barriers to Holy Friendship

We've spent the last several chapters exploring the joys and benefits of holy friendship. Some of the stories have hinted that participating in such intense, intimate, and vulnerable relationships can come at a cost. There are, of course, barriers to holy friendship, such as fear of vulnerability, lack of time, and our hypersexualized society. The pastors and leaders featured in this chapter address these barriers with conviction; thus, for the most part, their words do not need my interpretation.

Fear of Vulnerability

Marilyn, a pastor and practical theology professor, remembers,

> I did not really know how to be a friend until I was about twenty-five. Most of my relationships were me ministering to other people. My parents always said, "Look for the person who's lonely in the corner and befriend them." This did not make for mutual relationships.

The first time I had a real, true friend was in graduate school. My partner, Casey, and I were newly married, and we were struggling. Growing up in a pastor's home, we did not air our dirty laundry, so I felt trapped. I was afraid if I shared our challenges with someone, they would judge me or him. Feeling like I was out of options, I knew I had to be vulnerable with someone because I needed help.

One morning, I was meeting my friend Chris for coffee. I got in their car and just fell apart. I thought it might be wrong to share my struggles with them, and if it was, I would repent later. It was so hard for me to do. I was so lonely; I had to push through what I had been taught about keeping certain things hidden from view. I had to take the risk to find safety in our friendship. All these years later, we laugh at how nervous I was to "just be human" with them. At the time, I didn't know anything different [than to go it alone].

Marilyn's struggle pushed her to risk being vulnerable with a friend. Thankfully, her risk resulted in a lovely lifelong friendship. Another pastor, Lance, expressed his challenge in being vulnerable with a select few friends:

As a leader, I wrestle with how much of my inconsistencies and weaknesses I can afford to let show. Early in my ministry, I remember thinking that as a pastor, being vulnerable and revealing my shortcomings could diminish the message of Christ through me. Through time, therapy, and some periods of intense loneliness, I figured out I have to be totally real with some people, my inner circle. I have to choose these people wisely, but I have to have them. It's too lonely without them; I need the fellowship and transparency. And if I am not practicing vulnerability, how can I encourage it with others?

How Do You Make Time?

Look at your lunches. Who are you eating lunch with? Are you alone in your office doom-scrolling on your phone while you scarf down leftovers? If you bring your lunch from home, invite a friend to bring their lunch and meet in another room of your building, or their office, or a park, so you can talk. Support a locally owned restaurant by meeting a friend for lunch. What might happen to your friendships if you committed to having lunch with a friend once a month or once a week?

Finding Time

"How do you have time for your holy friendships?" young leaders often ask me as if I have a secret stash of time. "How do you have time for a demanding career, a young family, and robust friendships?" My answer is straightforward: I can't afford not to. Spending time with my holy friends is as critical to my health as good food, intellectual stimulation, or sleep. While I believe I could, I don't want to be married, a parent, or a minister without my friends by my side. Life is hard, and I don't want to do it by myself. I make time for friends because they are my life partners. My friends are so integrally stitched into the fabric of my everyday life, excluding them from my day equates to excluding one of my children or my spouse from it.

Spending time in conversation with my holy friends has such a powerful impact on my mood and behavior that my family can sense when I haven't spoken to one in a while. If I am particularly snappy or sad, my daughter is the first to ask, "When is the last time you talked or texted with Clara?" She knows my holy friends are a balm to my weary soul. Time with them is not a luxury; it is as necessary as breathing.

To the pastors and leaders who believe they don't have time to nurture friendships, that the work they are doing for their church or organization has to come first, I ask, "What is the cost of not spending time with your friends?" (I know you are out there—you folks who believe you are the exception to the rule.) The cost at the moment might not be noticeable; however, when a crisis arises or loneliness sets in, that is when we need our friends the most. But making or deepening friendships when we really need them is difficult. A ship's crew makes repairs and strengthens the ship when the seas are calm. If they wait until a storm is brewing and the ship begins taking on water, the work is infinitely more challenging. The time to cultivate and nurture our friendships is when our lives are going well, when we have time and energy to give and receive with someone else.

When I interviewed pastors and leaders for this book, I asked them what advice they would give to younger, emerging leaders about how to make time for holy friends. The majority of them recommended, "Do it when you are young and have more energy, resources, and time to commit to building relationships." When we are cultivating holy friendships, the beginning is the most time-intensive season of the relationship. Once a foundation is established, it can be built upon through virtual connections and face-to-face visits over time.

Come Stay with Me

My holy friends and I share our travel schedules with each other. If one of us is in a cool city for a few days and the timing works, we show up and share a room. We get our individual work done and hang out during our downtime. Getting to travel, doing work that fills my soul, and getting to be with a holy friend at the same time is the culmination of three of the things that support my flourishing.

The Optics of Holy Friendships

Not a lot of people know James and I are close friends. Our work takes us to the same cities a few times a year, where we pal around, sit together at events, and enjoy meals together. James and I are both clear about our platonic yet strong desire to spend time together and be active in each other's lives. We share a level of nonsexual intimacy in our conversations that is healthy, respectful, and holy. We delight in each other's company and are invested in each other's flourishing. I love him like a brother.

We have had some hilariously awkward conversations trying to articulate the external pressure we feel to prove to nosey onlookers that we are "just friends." Our intuition about "what others might think" subconsciously prompts us to keep our friendship low profile. Neither of us has anything to hide about our friendship, and yet we are aware of how easily people make assumptions about those in public-facing roles like ministry.

I admit I can speak only from my experience as a straight, cisgender woman when I spend time with a straight, cisgender man. I don't know what the optics are for LGBTQIA+ people and what assumptions are made when they spend quality time with someone of the same or opposite sex. But my observation is that church folks are especially guilty of hypersexualizing relationships between two people who are not married. Purity culture and sensationalized stories of the exploits of prominent leaders have brought scrutiny to relationships outside of monogamous Christian marriage. Such reactive responses to the irresponsible actions of a few people who do not behave in honorable ways complicate friendships for people like James and me.

Chemistry

Having chemistry between holy friends is normal. When you share a passion for something important to you, it is natural to feel drawn to them. That chemistry, that connection, however, does not mean you should alter your relationship. Having chemistry with someone doesn't mean you should marry them or have sex with them. It might mean you should embark on a project that will make a difference in your community or change the world together.

Some form of chemistry is present in all friendships; it is what pulls us together and provides a foundation upon which we can build a fruitful relationship. Society tries to convince us that chemistry equals sexual desire, which sadly sells friendship short.

My children say societal assumptions around opposite-sex relationships are relaxing. I hope they are right. Nonetheless, it is important to me that my children witness James's and my friendship as one of equals. I want them to see that two people can be healthy, holy friends who enjoy each other's company, share intimate and significant conversations, and rely on each other for beautiful, life-sustaining, nonsexual friendship. James helps me model for my kids that marriage is not the only way for two people to be in a committed relationship. We are showing them that healthy and holy friendships are worthy of our time, investment, and protection.

Other Barriers and Fears

The list of barriers to holy friendship includes fears around intimacy, competition, patriarchal systems, and wanting to avoid the pain of saying good-bye. I interviewed a number of pastors and Christian leaders in appointment systems or interim ministry settings who over time chose not to invest in friendships to avoid the pain of saying good-bye at the end of each one- or two-year appointment.

Change and transition are emotionally taxing. We saw this in chapter 5 with Heath and Andy. They enjoyed spending time together at their favorite coffee shop for over eight years. They both grieved and wondered what shape their friendship would take when one of them moved to a new town hours away. Over time, they figured out a communication rhythm that worked for them. The change was challenging but worth the effort because losing the friendship was not an option for them.

As I've said in previous chapters, a healthy and helpful way to deal with change and transition in friendships is to verbalize the significant role holy friends have had in our lives. And yet, even though I know this is true, it is often a challenge for me. Anyone who has spent more than five minutes with me knows I am rarely at a loss for words. However, I seem to forget how to speak when it comes time to say good-bye. In order to practice what I preach, I have to resist every urge in my body not to ghost at parties (disappear without telling anyone thank you for the invitation or good-bye). Please drop me off at the airport; don't come inside with me. I choose to love my friends deeply, so when one of them moves or our friendship transitions in some way, I have to figure out how to do the thing I hate the most. I have found, though, that words aren't the only way to express one's feelings or mark a transition in a friendship. Sometimes words can be offered alongside other forms of love and affirmation.

Max and I have known each other for twenty years and have worked together for the past six. There is an indentation in his old office doorframe where I have leaned my shoulder time and time again as I have sought his wise counsel, creative input, and consistent reminders of who I am and the work I am called to do. A conversation with him, and sometimes just a text thread, can change the way I see a challenge. I am a better human because of Max and his holy friendship.

When he announced he was leaving our workplace to dedicate his full-time energy to his growing consulting firm, I was gutted. It didn't matter that I saw it coming because he is good at what he does and I knew others would want him on their team. Covid-19 had already kept us out of the office and physically apart for eighteen months. I knew he was staying in town and we would stay in touch. I knew this wasn't the end of our friendship. And yet, I was deeply sad.

The week before Max's farewell party, I could think of little else. Social distancing accommodations made planning the event complicated, but the challenge provided even more motivation to ensure the party was a success. Everything about this event mattered to me. I may have even coached a few people on what to say in their toasts to make sure all the best sides of Max were addressed in a perfect mix of wit and whimsy.

Max came into the party space before it started. I set down whatever was in my hands and we hugged for a long time—one of those full-body hugs that makes you feel safe, known, and loved. I felt each of us take a big deep breath against the other's chest. "I'm sad," I whispered. "I know. Me too. And it's OK. This is supposed to be sad," he said.

The event was lovely. The toasts celebrated the best of Max and provided fodder for laughter and tears. It was perfect . . . except the end of the party meant it was time for Max to leave.

When I reflected with a friend about how important the success of the party was to me, I remember saying, "And it was all worth it because I love him."

She let my words soak in for a moment and said, "I wonder if the party was more for you than it was for Max." As someone known for being an excellent hostess, I was horrified at her statement. "That is ridiculous. It was for Max. He's leaving the office. He won't be there every day. I threw the party because I love him, and I wanted him to leave knowing he is loved and he will be missed." And with those words, I realized she was right. The party was about what I wanted and what I needed just as much as it was about Max.

Because of my close relationship with Max, I needed to put a pin in the continuum of our friendship that signified a shift in how we would be doing life together moving forward. I knew I would see him in a few weeks for lunch. I knew we would text each other about five different things before I went to sleep that evening. Still, I was sad. Our relationship was changing.

Thousands of leadership books acknowledge the discomfort of change. What I don't hear is language that could make change... more palatable? Easier to stomach? Less hard? We lack rituals and language around transition and relationships changing. Without effective ways to name our feelings around the hard work of acknowledging a change in a friendship, defaulting to ignoring or downplaying the significance of the moment can be more painful than the actual transition.

We need to acknowledge when we are sad and grateful with as much frequency as when we are happy. Since when is happiness the only appropriate feeling to express? I believe acknowledging and marking the transition from what was to what is now makes our friendship more resilient and adaptive. We can be honest with our emotions (with or without words), face hard things, and stick by each other in whatever comes next. It is what holy friends do for each other.

We might be tempted to ignore a transition to avoid the hurt. When we do that, however, we diminish the tremendous gift we are given in our friendships. We miss an opportunity to name and experience the beauty, generosity, love, and growth we enjoy in each other and imagine what shape the friendship might take next. But we and our holy friends deserve better. Our job as pastors and leaders is to nurture beloved community and help others experience the love and grace of God, thus we have to be about the work of removing or navigating around the barriers that keep this from happening.

The same is true for holy friendships. Holy friendships are one of God's gifts to us to experience beloved community and see God's love at work in one another. We need to support each other as we manage our fears and vulnerabilities. Changing the way our society looks at nonmarital friendships is a collective effort, deserving of our time and investment. And thanks be to God for technology for the ways it enables us to maintain precious friendships across great distances and time. I am convinced that for every barrier to holy friendships, there are twice as many reasons to pursue them. Their benefits far outweigh the costs and challenges. Holy friendships are always worth our energy, effort, emotional investment, and time because our flourishing in life and ministry is the goodness to which God calls us.

9

HOW DO I MAKE FRIENDS?

Searching for Connection

Before my daughter had a phone, when she wanted to play with the kids down the street, she would ask me to text their parents and see if her friends were available. Just about every time I would say, "Just go knock on their door and ask!" It was what I did as a kid. She would recoil in disgust and squeal, "No way! That's so awkward! What if the answer is no? Or what if they have other friends over? Or what if they don't want to play with me? Or what if their parents don't like me? I can't do that. Please, just text them." Most of the time, because I wanted thirty minutes of peace and quiet, I would text the neighbors and relay the answer to my daughter. Years later, I realize I did her, and the friends down the street, a disservice.

Approaching someone and asking if they want to play, talk, hang out, go for a walk, or spend time together is a life skill. Learning how to do this as a child is a rite of passage. By knocking on my friends' doors, I learned how to politely and clearly ask for what I wanted, to be patient, to listen, to suggest alternatives if I didn't get the answer I wanted, and most importantly, to face rejection and recover. By texting the parents of my daughter's friends, I was a buffer between her and her joy or disappointment in her desire to play. My desire for peace and quiet—and if I am honest, sometimes protecting my daughter from rejection—enabled her to postpone having to experience the vulnerability that comes with reaching out in friendship.

Now that she is older and has access to more forms of communication than I can fathom, she can use her phone in the same way I did for her: as a buffer against vulnerability and exposure. She can ask anyone to do anything without physically showing up, making eye contact, or using her voice; all she has to do is type into a screen. My daughter's experience is not unique. She is part of a generation of people who have the ability to connect with millions of others with the click of a button, and yet they tremble at the idea of verbalizing what they want and risking potential rejection.

I'm no longer surprised when younger leaders ask me how to find and cultivate holy friends. Sometimes the questioner is asking how to take a friendship with potential to the holy friendship level. Sometimes, though, leaders are asking literally where and how to make friends.

How do you make friends? You meet someone. You connect over something—a seminar topic, a favorite beach, a passion for motorcycles, or being too busy. Then you get curious. You ask them questions, listen to their answers, and then ask more questions. Smile. Make eye contact. Open up your body language to show you are engaged and listening. Laugh when they make a joke. Offer your own stories, and make it easy for the other person to ask you questions. Let the conversation run its course, and then tell them you enjoyed talking with them (if it is true). This is not creepy; it is a compliment. You are telling them they have something to offer and that you enjoyed learning about them and the interest you share. If it feels appropriate, say you'd enjoy talking again to follow up on something from the conversation.

Pray for Your Holy Friends

Pray for the friends you have not met yet just as you pray for the ones you already treasure in your life. Share with God the kind of friends you are seeking and ask for the Holy Spirit's guidance in finding and connecting with them.

Some folks ask me to back up a step and talk about where to actually find the people with whom you could possibly be friends. I've found a helpful way to respond is to take the questioner to one of my favorite places—the beach.

A few years ago, I went on a church retreat at the beach. (I think church retreats would be a lot more popular if they were always held at the beach!) Our family was new to the church, and we didn't know what to expect. A few women invited me to go on a walk. Except it wasn't really a walk. It was a shell hunt. Caswell Beach, North Carolina, has sections of beach that are inches deep with beautiful shells. I quickly learned about jingles, angel wings, turkey legs, lamb's ears, lady slippers, limpets, and olives.

Watching the women was amazing. Some of them were looking for specific shells for an art project. Others were happy to find anything interesting. I needed a walk or two, but eventually, I got pretty good at shell hunting. Successful shell hunting is all about knowing where to look and what to look for.

My family had been vacationing not far from Caswell for over a decade. The same shells have been there year after year, and yet only since that church retreat have I found the more rare and interesting shells native to the area. Nothing changed about the beach or the shells. I changed the way I look for them. Here's how to find a particular shell:

1. Know what you are looking for. If you are looking for general "shells," you will quickly become overwhelmed. In that case, it doesn't really matter what kind you are looking for. You can just pick one type for the day, and the next day you can look for another kind.

2. Do the research. Find out where your desired shell has been found in the past. Are there certain seasons or times of day when the tides are more likely to deposit your shell on the shore? I was able to gather most of this information from the women on the walk without asking many questions. They were giddy to see my growing interest in one of their passions and were eager to share everything they knew.

3. Look for your chosen shell in areas where there are lots of shells. Shells hang out with shells. Rarely will you find a specific shell just sitting alone in the sand. It can happen, but it is not likely.

4. Train your eyes to look for your shell. Shells won't just appear in front of you if you sit up by the sand dunes. Are you looking for a certain shape? Does it have a pattern? Is it flat or curved? Is it matte or shiny?

5. Be patient and pay attention. Sometimes the best shells are in ankle-deep water where the last of the baby waves are breaking. Move quickly if you think you see what you are looking for. If you find your shell, great! If not, appreciate the beauty and uniqueness of whatever you found and release it back to the water. It is likely the shell you found is the shell someone else is looking for.

6. Once you find your shell, look closely around it. Often, similar shells wash ashore when a nest of them has been disturbed on the ocean floor. Others like it might be nearby. If you need only one, enjoy the treasure you found. If you need a few, scoop them up, because you might find one that is more to your liking.

7. Be open to surprises. Once I was looking for olive shells with my daughter. We wanted to find about a hundred of them for a Christmas craft. Our eyes were trained to look for the slender, elongated shape, when a large round shark's eye shell rolled in the surf and hit my foot. I had never seen one that big, whole, and empty (without a critter living in it)! A prized find, it sits on my desk in my office. Sometimes the beach offers us undeserved and unsought gifts. Treasure them.

You've likely caught on by now. Finding friends is a lot like looking for shells. Let's look at the correlation:

1. Think about what kind of friend you are looking for. What do you want to be able to do together?

2. Ask yourself what you have to offer in a friendship. Do some introspection and get familiar with

your best traits and also your challenges. Knowing yourself well greatly increases your odds of being able to tell others about yourself.

3. Go where the kind of people you want to meet are. If you are frustrated with your work, don't look for friends in social settings with work people. Look for opportunities to be with people who enjoy topics and experiences you love that give you energy, spark ideas, and nurture creativity.

4. I have a friend who jokes that she is totally open to a romantic relationship. She is just waiting for the perfect person to show up on her doorstep (out of nowhere!). That is not how this works. Wishing and waiting gets no one any closer to a relationship. If you want to make a friend who shares your passion for your work, go to conferences. If you would like to watch and discuss movies, join a movie club. If you wish to appreciate art with a friend, attend a gallery opening. If you are looking to spend more time outside, walk around your neighborhood or local park and initiate conversations.

5. Keep an eye (and ear) out for the kind of friend you want to find. If you overhear someone ask an interesting question, casually join the conversation, and ask a follow-up question.

6. When you meet someone you think could be a potential friend, look for more in the same setting. You might only need one friend, or you might be looking for a few. Like attracts like.

7. Be open to finding a friend in an unusual setting. It happens, occasionally. (I know a pair of friends who met when one rear-ended the other's car.)

If at first you don't succeed, keep trying. If you email someone and invite them to lunch and they blow you off, don't worry about it. It is their loss. You are brave. You are friendly. If after meeting with someone a few times, you discover you don't really click, it is totally OK. Don't ghost them, but also don't agree to keep meeting. And when you make a friend, tell them what you appreciate about them. Thank them for being attentive and being a good listener (if that is true).

What Are You Looking For?

I've become fairly skilled at finding just about any kind of shell native to a particular beach. However, I cannot find a shark's tooth to save my life. I have friends who can walk alongside me and spot several shiny triangular teeth within a few moments while I stare blankly at the sand. My eyes are trained to look for shells, not teeth. Their eyes are trained to look for teeth, not shells.

I joined a Facebook group called Spot the Tooth. Skilled beach combers post pictures of shark teeth they spot in the sand before they pick them up. I'm getting pretty good at spotting the teeth without having to "cheat" and scroll down to the pictures with the teeth circled for those who cannot spot them or give up.

I wonder what a similar practice might look like for spotting potential friends. Where would you look, and what attributes would indicate you were on the right track?

In my experience and as I observe others, I find point 3 is key. I think about Brian, a longtime pastor who, when he started out in ministry, loved going to his denomination's national and regional gatherings. They were places of synergy, collaboration, joy, and relationship building. Over time, the meetings were increasingly dominated by laborious political discussions and arguments about depleting resources. He grew tired of the same conversations with the same people who saw little hope for the future. Attending those gatherings took energy away from him. He stopped attending because he knew he needed to be with people who were passionate about similar things—like the neighborhood surrounding the church.

Brian began going for walks in his church's neighborhood and got to know his neighbors. He asked questions, and he listened well. He learned who was passionate about what. He figured out who should be connected to who and introduced them. His church hosted block parties so neighbors could meet other neighbors. By refocusing his energy on what was life-giving, Brian not only made new friends; he also created space for other relationships to develop.

Look for friends in places that bring you and others joy. If you look for friends in places you begrudgingly *have* to be, you are likely to find others who are there for the same begrudging reason. While this environment can provide opportunities for cathartic cynicism, do you really want to begin a friendship rooted in something that doesn't spark joy in you? Find your joy, and look for friends there.

If You Want It, Ask for It

While I was interviewing leaders for this book, I was arranging an appointment with a good friend. I timidly asked, "Do you think your spouse would want to talk to me?"

By reputation, Emily is relational, funny, smart, compassionate, thoughtful, brave, and creative. We are about the same age, have kids the same age, and we know a lot of the same people within our work. I sensed she had all the ingredients to become a friend—maybe eventually, a holy friend—and I had already met her twice, briefly. Each time, we fell quickly into great conversations about our interests, our families, and the challenges of our current season of life. After we met the first time, I finished reading a book in my hotel room that night so I could give it to her the next day. I raved about it when we talked, and she said she had heard of it but was waiting to hear some reviews from "real people." With my recommendation, she was eager to read it.

Emily graciously agreed to give me some of her time, and we chatted for fifteen minutes before I realized I needed to shift the conversation to holy friendships, our agreed-upon topic. We could have talked for much longer. Our conversation was deep, personal, and intimate. She has had a number of life experiences dramatically different from mine. She opened my eyes to a number of alternative perspectives. At the appointed time, I began wrapping up the interview and said, "I've really enjoyed this. I like talking with you and want to make our paths cross in the future, because I feel like we could be good friends." I paused, hoping she didn't think I was weird. "Me too!" she replied. Her face lit up. "I would love that. I totally agree. When we can travel more, let's make it happen." "Great," I said, relieved and excited.

I don't know if Emily and I will meet in person. I hope we will. Her response to my question seemed genuine. Honestly, I would not typically have been that vulnerable or forward with someone I had just met. We already had a foundation for a possible friendship because of our two previous interactions and my friendship with her spouse. But my learning from this experience, whether or not Emily and I become friends, is that sometimes when we see something we want, we have to ask for it.

When Someone Says No, It's Not You

Every once in a while, I'll reach out to someone I would like to get to know and they will decline. Years ago, I saw the potential for a friendship with someone connected to my work. I sent an email that was casual and noncommittal—a simple invitation to get out of the office and share thirty minutes or an hour getting to know each other. She replied to my email, "I have a lot going on these days, and I really don't have the bandwidth for any more friends right now."

I was flabbergasted. I wasn't asking for one of her organs. I was asking for a little time over coffee. After I regained my senses, I was (mostly) grateful for her honesty. She was in a busy season, which I could certainly understand. She also communicated that she had the friendships she needed and didn't have the energy for more at the moment. Her response was about her, not me. Upon reflection, I respect her response. While I don't think she needed to be as blunt as she was, she set a powerful example for me to follow should I find myself in a similar situation. Her response hasn't stopped me from inviting others out for coffee or trying to get to know new people. If anything, receiving her email taught me that such rejection is easily survivable. The good news is, far more of my invitations have been accepted than declined. I am certain you will have that experience too.

Back to the beach for a moment. One year, my family went to the beach for a cold, windy week in the spring. Walking along the beach was ideal because in the off-season, tourists aren't there, and most of the locals choose not to brave unpleasant weather. The best part of that trip, however, was the shell hunting. The local government was renourishing the beach after a hurricane wiped most of it out six months earlier. They were pumping sand from the ocean floor about half a mile out onto the beach. The "new" sand was full of shells we had never seen before or that we had only seen in bits and pieces. (Yes, it destroyed some sea life because it disturbed some underwater animal habitats, but it also provided a much better nourished and safer beach.) We collected bags full of rare and beautiful shells we still talk about and display in our home.

My point is, sometimes the stars align, and you find yourself in the right place at the right time for finding the most amazing shells and/or making incredible friends. This happened for me when I was invited to teach in a seminary certificate program tangentially connected to my work (or so I thought).

Practice Sabbath

It may sound countercultural, but once I fully embraced the habit of a weekly Sabbath, my relationships strengthened and became more fulfilling. By stopping to delight in the goodness and abundance of God, I found myself wanting to be with others who did the same. In community, we rest, reflect, and renew our relationships with God and one another.

I knew at the end of the first day that some of the people I met would be lifelong friends. We were in a crucible moment—away from our everyday stressors and responsibilities. We were surrounded by brilliant scholars, pastors, and practitioners who wanted to be there to learn from one another and share their expertise with emerging leaders. We had ample free time to mix and mingle in between low-pressure opportunities to meet people. I left with a handful of friends. I was hopeful that with regular but casual communication and sustained conversations over time, we would become holy friends. I worked to secure an invitation to return to the event for several years. Eventually, I didn't need the event to anchor the friendships. They matured into holy friendships we could sustain on our own—although, I'll never turn down an occasion to revisit a place that birthed so many beautiful holy friendships.

When you find yourself in one of these rare crucible moments, pay attention. Have a second cup of coffee with the interesting person. Walk the long way to the next meeting to keep the conversation going. Stay up way too late to continue swapping stories. And skip the meetings or events that are less important than cultivating friendships. (By the way, that is *all* the meetings.)

I went to the beach for most of my life without noticing the incredible shells that were beneath my feet. I saw them, but I had to learn to recognize their value and the unique characteristics of each one. Making friends is similar. Sometimes we don't see what is right in front of us until we invest the time and energy into figuring out who we can be as a friend and what attributes we are looking for in a friend. And the best news is, the beach is new with every tidal change. God is always creating new opportunities for us to meet new people, cultivate friendships, and flourish in our ministries.

10

How Can I Help Others Have Them?

Cultivating the Conditions

Once we know the value and benefit of holy friendship, our imagination opens to what is possible if our parishioners, constituents, and community members have these life-sustaining relationships. We can envision communities of healthy and flourishing leaders who desire to work together to be the hands and feet of God in the world. So how do we cultivate environments that are ripe for developing significant relationships? Some institutions have traditions and practices we can learn from and adapt to our individual contexts today.

As I sat in the last session of my freshman orientation at a small liberal arts college, the president addressed the new students and many of the accompanying parents in a crowded chapel. He said, "Parents, look around. There is a good probability that your child's in-laws are in this room. This weekend, you very well might be meeting the people with whom you will spend future family holidays." Everyone laughed and looked around the room sheepishly. I took him seriously. My parents met in the student union on that very campus and got married twenty-two years earlier in the chapel where we sat.

The president could make such a statement because he had the evidence: people like my parents and many others across generations of students and alumni. He knew the conditions were present in the four-year undergraduate experience for compatible people to meet, fall in love, and make plans to pursue life together. The combination of being away from home, enjoying newfound independence, encountering different experiences and people, and facing the challenges and opportunities of rigorous academic studies contributes to the conditions for long-term relationships to flourish.

As leaders, we need to ask deeper questions about the ecologies in which we live and the institutions to which we give our precious time, energy, and resources. How is our work helping people flourish? How can we cultivate communities and institutions in which more people can discover the significance of holy friendships and offer such friendships to others? Pastors and other Christian leaders can play powerful roles in cultivating the conditions for human flourishing within churches and other Christian institutions.

Institutions cannot exhibit the attributes of friendship, but their leaders can affect how employees, members, and constituents cultivate holy friendships in a number of ways. Leaders can create the conditions for holy friendships to form, grow, and thrive.

They can affirm holy friendships and the numerous benefits that come from caring deeply about those with whom we live, work, and play. Imagine the kind of leaders a community would attract, develop, and deploy if it valued and supported holy friendships. Imagine the impact a community and all those connected to it could make.

The Gathering and Galileo Church, both in the Dallas–Fort Worth area of Texas, are two churches making strides in prioritizing friendships as pillars of their churches. I asked Katie, the pastor at Galileo Church, and Irie, one of the pastors at the Gathering, how they create Christian community that nurtures relationships and holy friendships. They explained:

> **Katie:** At Galileo Church, we are building infrastructure where friendship can happen. I can't make people be friends. I can't magically give you friends. But I can build some infrastructure, meaning a light schedule of small groups, eating and drinking together, and plenty of money to do that so nobody's worried about providing dinner for all their friends.
>
> Within that structure, we can introduce some processes where friendships can flourish. For instance, I developed a game that teaches leaders how to facilitate different kinds of conversation in a small group so that people, if they want to, feel comfortable, share appropriately, and lay a foundation for friendship.
>
> The pandemic really tested this. The infrastructure fell apart because we couldn't gather. But the friendships remain. I kept saying to people, "We didn't want this experiment, but here it is. Do the friendships

remain when the infrastructure is gone?" And thanks be to God, they do. A lot of people discovered that they were actually friends even when the church couldn't call them together.

When we pay attention to the Gospels, we see that Jesus is always putting people into relationship, whereas I think the kind of church programming I learned how to do doesn't do that. It is about how many butts are in the seats. This means we have to recognize we are not just changing our programming. We have to change what we are measuring too. What if instead of measuring church by attendance, tithes, or baptisms, we asked, "Did you feel seen today? Did you see anybody else today in a new way with new eyes? Were you curious about anyone?" What if we actually got curious about one another? We can do this when we make space for people to be with each other and nurture friendships.

Irie: Creating these kinds of spaces is rooted in the leadership of the church and community. You have to have leaders who believe in the power of healthy relationships and have the courage to model what they look like. There has to be space for each person to live their truth without judgment. That doesn't mean everyone just does their own thing. It means cultivating a community, a space where there is respect for difference, for freedom. And with freedom comes responsibility. We are each other's keepers, so we don't want to do harm, and we want to hold one another accountable to our shared values.

We need to create spaces where everyone can find and use their voice. Usually at church, we are quiet until we are told to sing or say something specific that someone else picked out for us. Someone else tells us when and how to move. We need to provide opportunities for people's voices to be heard and invite them to tell their stories. We have to help our people find their people.

Katie: As we help our people figure out who their people are, leaders have to model and churches need to cultivate spaces where disagreements can happen with respect and love. We let disagreements fester so easily, and they tear relationships and churches to pieces. Too often, the church suffers from toxic politeness—people worrying that disagreeing with someone else will hurt their feelings or make them uncomfortable. What do you think Jesus and the rabbis were doing in the temple? They were talking, agreeing and disagreeing, and figuring out how to interpret the Scriptures in their community.

Irie: The church has to be a safe place for hard conversations. Everyone's voice should be heard in love and respect. We don't raise our voices. We take turns. We listen well. And we can agree to disagree. It is acceptable within our congregation to end a conversation with

> opposing views as long as we remain friends
> and we don't leave when things get hard.
> This takes courage and trust from the leaders
> and the members.

Irie and Katie are exploring and experimenting their way into alternative ways of cultivating and nurturing beloved community in their congregations. They are discerning habits and practices, specific to their individual contexts, that create a sacred space for their congregants to make connections, share stories, and mutually support one another. As fairly young churches (less than ten years old), they are weaving friendship and life-giving relationships into the institutional DNA of their communities.

Sunday School and Small Groups

Some of what Irie and Katie are doing in their churches may sound familiar. You might be thinking, That sounds a lot like Sunday school. We've been doing that for years. Some Sunday school classes and small groups can be fertile ground for cultivating relationships and holy friendships, depending on the leadership.

Professor Emeritus Keith Drury at Indiana Wesleyan University would ask his Christian education students, "If you have an hour and a half for adult Sunday school, how much time should be left free for adults to just talk and offer prayer requests?" Students typically guessed between five and fifteen minutes. Keith always stunned the budding ministers with this observation: "Half. Half of the class should be unstructured with space for people to talk, share food, and voice prayer requests. Do not try to rush people to get to the curriculum, because whatever is in the study guides isn't nearly as important as the time they spend together. They need each other. Their lives are so busy, and this may be the only time they stop to breathe with others, listen, and reflect. So stay out of their way, trust them, and the Holy Spirit. Create the space and let them fill it."

Leading Sunday school classes and small groups in ways that promote friendship and relationship building requires mature, differentiated, and self-aware teachers and facilitators who are trained and supported by a leadership team who has a vision for relationship building as part of spiritual formation. These leaders know how to create safe spaces for people to share, tell the truth, struggle, actively listen, and be open to learning new and different ways God is working in and through other people. Vulnerability, empathy, compassion, and mediation skills are also helpful.

Entrepreneurial church starters beginning microchurches —smaller congregations meeting in homes that are limited to a certain number of members before they split into a new microchurch—often embody some of the conditions needed to cultivate holy friendships. The sense of mutuality among the members is particularly strong, as everyone brings something to the service in a shared-leadership model. Intentionally avoiding traditional hierarchical leadership structures, members create fluid and adaptive practices and worship experiences that mirror their individual and collective faith journeys. Such environments are ripe for creating and nurturing holy friendships because of the way they encourage sharing stories, putting faith into action in the community, and valuing what everyone brings to the experience.

Crucible Experiences

Eli and I knew each other socially before we embarked on a three-week mission immersion trip to Kenya. We were on the other side of the world where we did not speak the native languages, and everything was different: the food; the (ahem) facilities; the landscape, daily habits, and expectations; and how we experienced time.

After a particularly exhausting day in the Masai Mara and consuming some unusual (to us) food, I collapsed from exhaustion in the tent I was sharing with Eli. As I faded off to sleep, I could hear my trip-mates talking around the fire and who knows what kinds of noises behind them.

I woke up with a rush of adrenaline, swearing I heard baboons beating on the outside of our tent. They were loud and angry. In terror, I rolled over to check on Eli. She was gone. The baboons had taken her. How could I sleep through something like that? I could still hear them beating on the outside of our tent, but I knew I had to alert the others so we could look for Eli. I put on my shoes and unzipped the tent to orient myself to the rest of the camp. I saw the fire with a few people still sitting around it. How did they not hear the baboons? How could they sit there as if nothing had happened?

I perched on the balls of my feet, tore open the tent, and ran as fast as I could to the fire, hoping I was faster than the baboons. Terrified, but knowing I had to try to save Eli, I yelled to the others as I neared the fire. "Eli! Eli! They've got Eli! The baboons! They . . ."

Everyone around the fire stared at me with worried looks on their faces. And then Eli turned around and smiled at me. It turns out what I thought were the baboons was the wind beating against the walls of our tent. I had been asleep for only a few minutes. Eli had never come to bed. She was at the fire the entire time. I was embarrassed and relieved. Eli stood up and hugged me tightly, saying, "I'm sorry you are scared. I love you for trying to outrun the baboons to save me. I'll never forget that!"

Throughout the remainder of the trip, we experienced many other memorable moments that became more powerful because of the way our friendship changed that night. We trusted each other more quickly, shared more generously, and appreciated each other and our strange and beautiful surroundings all the more. We saw the movement of the Holy Spirit and God's love more clearly because our friendship deepened in such a palpable way.

Neither one of us has ever forgotten that crucible experience. It bonded us together in a friendship unlike what we have with anyone else. We have come and gone in and out of each other's lives a few times since that fateful trip. I trust Eli with my life, and I know she does the same. She is one of the few people who has seen me physically terrified, helpless, threatened, and vulnerable. I, on the other hand, realized the treasure I had in her as a friend when I thought I had lost her in such a violent and traumatic way. We can go without seeing each other for a while and pick up wherever we left off with relative ease. There is something about experiencing a crucible with another person that enables them to see a side of us that others may not. The crucible gave us a deep foundation for a lasting holy friendship.

Churches and Christian institutions offer many opportunities for people from different walks of life to step out of their comfort zones and experience something new together. Serving in soup kitchens, picking up trash on the side of a highway, going on mission trips, traveling on learning journeys, taking classes together, leading a group with someone—all of these are opportunities to experience crucible moments that can lay the groundwork for holy friendships to bloom.

The Power to Bless

The church has significant power to validate and bless relationships (and on the dark side, withhold blessing, for which we are watching denominations split in half). Historically, most of this power comes in the form of weddings, blessing new partners in life and new families forming. Other blessing practices are baby dedications, baptisms, and confirmations, when the church welcomes new members into the assembled community. Parents, guardians, and families are blessed and charged with the spiritual formation of the one being dedicated, baptized, or confirmed. Sometimes significant anniversaries or retirements merit flowers at the altar, a dedication in the bulletin, and perhaps a reception in a fellowship hall.

While churches help us celebrate a number of milestones and relationships, they fall silent about the most prevalent form of relationship in their midst: friendship. How might the church encourage relationships other than marriage? How could a beloved community acknowledge, validate, and celebrate mutual, healthy, life-giving holy friendships?

Pastor Mike Mather at First United Methodist Church in Boulder, Colorado, laments the opportunities the church is missing in not publicly acknowledging the power of friendship within our congregations. He explains,

I was at a humanitarian award ceremony last year. The honoree had tremendous power and considerable resources. Colleagues listed all the incredible acts of service this generous man had performed in his community. When it was his turn to speak, he used the time to name and thank his friends who had contributed to all the work for which he was being celebrated. He said his efforts had nothing to do with his money or influence. His real power was in his friendships. Shame on us [the church] for that happening in a civic center. That should be our work. The church needs to be doing that. We should be celebrating friendship and the amazing work that happens among friends.

I know of a church where during the announcements, the congregation recognizes not only people's belly-button birthdays but their sobriety birthdays. They lift up second chances and new life and affirm the hard work that goes into sobriety. Celebrating it in church marks it as holy. There is power in that. The church has the power to bless, and we hold on to that power like it will disappear if we use it.

We create liturgies for things we care about, such as sobriety. What if we had occasions to celebrate friendships in worship? What if we talked about where we see friendships blossoming and named them as holy? What if we laid hands on friends and blessed them? We bless backpacks and animals. Why aren't we blessing these precious relationships at the center of our lives? The church has the power to do this.

We need to tell stories of friendship. They are all around us if we are paying attention, and the church needs to pay attention. We need to acknowledge and celebrate the healthy, fruitful, and purposeful friendships happening in our midst. It's like sunlight. The more light we shine on a field, the more it grows.

Mike's challenge to pastors and Christian leaders can provoke powerful and system-shifting changes in congregations and organizations. Want to improve morale within your church? Ask people to talk about their friendships. Want to have a healthier, well-differentiated staff? Talk to your staff about your holy friendships. Don't bore them with details, but mention when you are spending time with one of these friends. Even simple ways of modeling holy friendship can encourage it for those paying attention. Want to grow your young adult ministry? Millennials and Generation Z are partnering up later in life, if at all. They are looking and longing for deep and meaningful relationships outside of traditional Christian marriage. Figure out a way to cultivate spaces where holy friendships can be nurtured and thrive, and watch people show up. (Hint: These spaces will likely not be in the four walls of your church; you need to go to where they are.)

Be a Matchmaker

When new people come into your orbit, imagine who they might pair well with in a friendship. Introduce them in a way in which conversation can flow easily and they can spend time together. Tell them both why you think they could be friends; people love hearing what others see in them. Hearing it from their spiritual leaders is especially meaningful.

The church has a tremendous opportunity to be a place where people gather across generations for learning, sharing, listening, trusting, and living together. As a society, we are yearning for safe conversations about things that matter to us deeply and yet divide us. Pastors and other Christian leaders are poised to convene these kinds of conversations, to daily bring people together for the sake of relationships, the community, and the work of the gospel. We need to lean into our underutilized power to cultivate the conditions for meaningful conversations, build trust, and acknowledge the incredible life-sustaining power of holy friendships for individual and communal flourishing. We can do this significant work by focusing our attention on not just our individual stories but those of our community and God's overarching story of love and redemption.

Pastors and other Christian leaders spend a lot of time discerning the needs of their communities so their church or organization might address them and be a good neighbor. But are we really listening? The statistics on loneliness, isolation, depression, and loss of purpose demand that we pay attention to what our neighbors are saying but we may not be hearing. Our communities are asking for safe spaces for meaningful conversation, people who will tell the truth and share in their vulnerability, and ultimately, friendship.

The Power and Platform to Bless

My friend Amy, a pastor in an urban church, was covertly listening to her young adult daughter and her friends talk about friendship. Spencer Sleyon, a twenty-two-year-old Black rapper and producer from East Harlem, casually said, "My best friend is an eighty-one-year-old white woman who lives in a retirement community in Florida."[1] Amy was instantly hooked into the conversation.

Spencer explained that he had cultivated a friendship with Rosalind Guttman, a woman he had been randomly paired up with in the game *Words with Friends*. They had played more than three hundred games and began using the game's chat function to discuss current events and Spencer's plans for the future. Ros encouraged Spencer to be bold and go for his dreams.

Amy knew there could be more to the story, so she contacted Ros and set up a time for her and Spencer to fly to Palm Beach. They shared only an afternoon together, but the chemistry between Spencer and Ros was so easy. Amy recalls they seemed to be magnetically drawn to each other. Before they got on the plane to return to New York, Spencer tweeted a few pictures and a brief synopsis of his experience. When he landed, his tweet had been liked more than a million times, had been shared almost a quarter of a million times, and had collected more than five thousand comments—enough to get the attention of national news outlets. The world clearly wanted to hear their story.[2]

Amy used her pastoral platform to enable Ros and Spencer's friendship to become an embodied reality. She saw a way to bless Ros and Spencer and helped make their visit possible. Their story, in turn, highlighted a lovely relationship that inspired millions of people who liked Spencer's tweet, read the *New York Times* article, or shared the Facebook post.

Without that trip to Florida, Ros and Spencer's connection likely would not have enjoyed an experience of person-to-person flourishing. Amy's acknowledging, encouraging, and blessing of Spencer and Ros's friendship changed their lives, and the world caught a glimpse of beauty and friendship in a most unlikely way. From the number of posts and retweets, the world is yearning for examples of connection and friendship. Pastors have tremendous power to notice, affirm, bless, and offer a platform for meaningful stories of friendship the world is begging to hear.

Pastors and Christian leaders, you can harness your power and use it for good, leading your institutions in ways that cultivate the conditions for holy friendships to grow and flourish. Nurturing these communities is a large part of the work we are called to do as we grow Christian disciples, encourage beloved community, and help one another live into the people God is creating us to be. Once you know the power of holy friendships, use your imagination, and interrogate your spaces and practices. Challenge your leadership to cultivate communities in which holy friendships flourish, and you will in turn see your ministries and communities flourish.

How Do We Model Holy Friendships?

Recognizing God at Work

When I teach about holy friends, I show a slide with pictures of myself and some of my holy friends. I want people to see who I am talking about—that holy friends are not a framework, theory, suggestion, or luxury. They are a necessity. I cannot be the leader I need and want to be without them. Showing others that I have flesh-and-blood holy friends gives them permission to seek out holy friendships for themselves. I believe it is critical for supervisors, mentors, and those in leadership to model healthy relationships—to (literally) name their holy friends and talk about the impact spending time with them has on their lives. Hearing a mentor or boss talk about their holy friends and seeing them be a holy friend to others gives emerging leaders permission to invest in similar relationships. In many ways, our modeling holy friendships for others is an aspect of leadership development. By setting the example of healthy holy friendships, we cultivate the conditions for others to seek out holy friendships for mutual flourishing.

A young pastoral leader confided to me that she was worried she'd be considered "unproductive" if she "got caught" spending time with someone in what appeared to be a social engagement during normal working hours. "When I have a lunch or coffee scheduled on a weekday with a friend, I mark it 'private' on my calendar, and if anyone asks, I say I'm meeting with a colleague," she told me. "In this season when budgets are tight and cutbacks are necessary, I can't afford to give anyone a reason to think I am not working."

This raises a question that plagues pastoral leaders. What is work? How should pastoral leaders be spending their time? Who gets to decide what counts as work, what is worth our time? What does "being productive" mean for pastors and Christian leaders who are called to the highly relational work of building community for the sake of the gospel, work that necessitates our cultivating and nurturing holy friendships to sustain us?

The last few years dealing with the Covid-19 pandemic have taught us that most of us don't do well in isolation. When we are lonely, not only does our health suffer; so do our creativity, productivity, resilience, and dedication. Our commitment to our vocations requires that we carve out space and time for holy friends who help us feel less alone, encourage us in our work, boost our creativity, bolster our resilience, remind us of our role in God's ongoing work in the world, and help us live into God's calling for us.

I tried to communicate to the young leader that we are called to spend whatever time, resources, and energy we need to sustain ourselves in our work. Spending time with our holy friends is part of our work because it contributes to our personal and professional flourishing, which enables our congregation and/or community to flourish. Healthy pastors lead healthy churches.

My heart breaks knowing she feels like she has to keep her coffee engagements private for fear that she'll be perceived as not working. If she returns to the office physically, emotionally, and spiritually recharged, then that meeting is part of her work. If her sermons, Bible studies, lessons, newsletters, and meetings are better because she's had coffee with friends, then that (or whatever else she does to improve them) is the work she is supposed to be doing.

I share this young woman's story to catch the eye of pastors and other leaders with staff working alongside them. Part of our responsibility as effective Christian leaders is to both model and encourage holy friendship among our staff and leadership teams. This is not another item on our staff's job description but rather an affirmation of their humanity and their need for holy friendship. It will also help them do their work better, which helps you do your work better.

Imagine how different the young woman's ministry might be if she worked with a leader who knows and affirms the value of holy friendship. Modeling holy friendship can be as easy as casually mentioning these relationships are important to us. Pastors should not underestimate the power of referring to their friendships in sermons and Bible studies. Displaying pictures of friends in our office communicates that we value relationships beyond our family. Our staff, volunteers, constituents, and congregants are paying attention and will follow our lead. Modeling holy friendship is a critical way both to hold ourselves accountable to practices of friendship and to lead others to health and flourishing.

Modeling for Children
and Families

One of the most significant by-products of my work on holy friendship is the way it has changed how I parent my two children. My kids are paying attention. For young people to cultivate healthy holy friendships, first they must see how necessary they are through our modeling. I want them to see how I value my holy friends as family and treasure them as gifts from God. I want them to nurture their own friendships for the joy, support, challenge, and love they will experience from them. I want them to have friends who will be with them without reservations. I want to teach them well so they can experience the flourishing that comes from holy friendship and enable that flourishing among others.

I also want my children to grow up knowing that just as we live into our faith in community, we also lead in community. They are learning that their pastor-parents do not carry out their ministries in isolation. The number of pastor's kids (PKs) I interviewed who can't remember their parents having friends as they were growing up is staggering. Many blamed the lack of friends on the busyness of ministry while raising children and dealing with the other pressures that come with midlife. Others recall the competitive nature of denominational politics. And many critique the church's social and power structures for prohibiting friendships between clergy and laity.

Kids know when their parents are flourishing or languishing. They can sense our job satisfaction, fulfillment, or indifference. My children know vocational ministry is challenging. Mark and I know we cannot lead in isolation and, moreover, that we would never want to do ministry alone. We regularly tell the kids stories about how our holy friends help us with both monumental decisions and mundane annoyances that arise in our work. My spouse and I also talk openly with them about how our family makes certain sacrifices because God has called the two of us, and our family, to full-time ministry. They understand that our choices affect how we do our work.

I introduced you to my holy friends Hannah and Evangeline in chapter 5. Hannah and Evangeline have nurtured their relationship as both sisters and holy friends.

Evangeline is an incredibly strong and brave woman who left her twenty-eight-year abusive marriage a few days before Christmas. My kids and spouse love Evangeline and felt deeply for her and her family. When I told them I needed to spend a few days with her, they not only understood that I needed to go; they offered their help too. Knowing I had their support and fierce love behind me enabled me to leave them in such a busy time for our family to love on another family.

Hannah and I were by her side to help her figure out the next steps, to find an apartment, and to tend to all the details that come with such a crisis. Holy friends showed up with a truck and muscle power to move furniture. Others mailed pots, pans, plates, towels, batteries, flashlights—everything one needs to establish a household but doesn't necessarily remember in the moment. We spent four hard and beautiful days putting together closet racks, shopping, wrapping gifts, making lists, and sometimes just sitting in silence. It was not the ramp-up to Christmas any of us expected or wanted, and yet we wouldn't have been anywhere else.

A few days later back at home, my family celebrated Christmas with fewer gifts, not-so-fancy food, and a bit less fanfare than we usually do. And it was fine. I was so grateful to have the four of us around the tree, knowing how quickly things can change. The day after Christmas, an envelope arrived addressed to my spouse and children. It read,

Dear Mark, Ava, and Owen,

I am sure that getting through these last busy days before Christmas without Victoria / Mom last week was hard. I just want to thank the three of you for lending her to help Evangeline. Sometimes life gets really hard. I don't know how people do it without our friends who are family.

I am grateful to you three for being part of the team helping Evangeline through. You guys are awesome! So much love and thanks, Hannah

I can tell my children a thousand stories trying to convey how much my friends mean to me and how important they are in my life. Hannah did it in a few sentences, and she acknowledged their part in the story about what showing up for a friend means.

The love, trust, and support among Hannah, Evangeline, and me are fierce. So is our awareness that our relationships are literal lifesavers. This story shows, though, why it is so important that we talk about our holy friendships with our children, spouses, and significant others. In this case, our families know we are important to one another, that we make one another stronger, smarter, more creative, more adaptive, and better at being parents, siblings, children, and partners in our nuclear families. When my nuclear family supports my holy friendships, everyone benefits.

Lizzy, a Christian leader and mother of three young adult children, reflected similarly:

Modeling healthy friendships and encouraging them among my kids is front and center in my parenting. I believe it is central to their survival because of the isolation and loneliness that we're seeing all around us, which has been magnified during Covid-19. We emphasize the importance of stitching together your chosen family and investing your time in others. And we try to help them as we can, opening our home to all their friends. We make pounds and pounds of chicken wings and thousands of pounds of chocolate-chip cookies because that's what the seventeen-year-olds like.

The kids saw this come to fruition when their chosen family showed up for them at their grandfather's funeral. It was a great teaching moment to say, "This is why we nurture friendships. When you invest in each other, your friends show up for you."

Also, as our kids are getting ready to launch, we want them to keep friendships at the forefront of their planning. We have gone so far as to say, "Even if it costs you a grade, show up for your friends. If you miss studying for an exam because you showed up for your friend's grandfather's funeral, in the long run, that is your priority." They may not understand why we prioritize this now, but that wisdom will come with time.

The way Min Jee, a pastor and mother of three, experienced friendships growing up shapes the way she encourages friendship among her children:

Friendship was weird for me. We had close family relationships, and we participated in a local church. Church was where we experienced helpful relationships outside of family. School was for learning, not for making friends. It wasn't until high school that I began bringing friends into our home, which my parents tolerated but were not thrilled about. They preferred we focus on familial relationships and school.

This is probably why I work so hard to encourage playdates with my children and their friends. I'm constantly offering to organize events for them and take them places to meet up with others. They don't seem to want my help. "Mom! You can't force friends on us! Let us do it on our own" is something they have said more than once.

It's important to me that the kids know how important friendship is. I want them to know that friendship can be just as significant a relationship as a marriage, a parent-child bond, or other traditional human connection. Most expressions of Christianity hold up monogamous Christian marriage—which produces children, thus a family—as the ultimate model of a relationship. It is as if "be fruitful and multiply," rather than loving God and one's neighbor, is the greatest commandment.

Friendship can help prepare us for marriage, helping us discern what we want in a spouse and how to be the best partner we can be to them once we find them. But I want the kids to know they have options, beyond traditional marriage, for healthy relationships. I believe friendship offers them lots of different ways to be in relationship with others.

Who, then, might need to see you model holy friendship? Who might need to see holy friendship at work in order to feel they have permission to pursue such life-giving relationships?

When I think about the young leader at the beginning of this chapter, I wonder who she might be and what she could accomplish in her ministry if she were supported by a leader who values and models holy friendships. As leaders mentoring the next generation, it is our responsibility to equip them with the tools and resources they need to flourish. Our having holy friendships and modeling them for others cultivates an environment that brings us closer to God's beloved community.

Modeling God at Work

My holy friend Carmelle has the gift of noticing the presence of God in big and small moments. Her Pentecostal Miami Haitian upbringing prompts her to shout "Yes, Lord" and "Amen" as she follows the movement of the Holy Spirit in all her conversations and interactions. Sometimes I feel as if I am listening to a preacher rise to a crescendo when she shakes her head and says, "Humph. Look at God."

> A loved one is healed from an illness. Look at God.
> Someone is struggling and by grace is still making it. Look at God.
> An innovative idea arises out of two strangers having a conversation. Look at God.
> I lay my head down to sleep in my safe and comfortable home. Look at God.
> A holy friend walks alongside another through the valley of the shadow of death. Look at God.

Carmelle's proclamation, I believe, is at the core of holy friendship. Holy friends walk alongside us in all the ups, downs, and boring normality of life and redirect our attention to God.

One of the most gratifying gifts of doing the research for this book has been glimpsing the breadth and depth of holy friendships among those I interviewed. I left every conversation overwhelmed with awe and wonder at the enumerable ways God is at work through holy friendships. Sometimes speechless with gratitude, often all I can say is, "Look at God!"

One of my goals in researching and writing this book was to provide snapshots of diverse pastors and leaders who rely on their holy friends to sustain them and help them grow and flourish in a variety of contexts. I hope their stories inspire what is possible for you and those who walk alongside you in your vocation. My desire is to contribute to the larger ongoing conversation of what it means for humans to flourish.

I remember the moment I recognized that this book needs to exist. I was leading a retreat for youth ministers and planned to list holy friendships as one of several ways to nourish their well-being and contribute to vocational vitality. The energy in the room changed when I described holy friendships. They asked questions and shared examples. Some wanted me to validate that what they had were, indeed, holy friendships. Others expressed grief in not having them but wanting to cultivate them. I never got to talk about the other items on my list. The ministers took the idea of holy friendships and ran with it. By the end of the evening, #holyfriendship was shorthand for "I've got your back" and "We're in this together." They recognized the significance of their friends, but more importantly, they knew how their holy friends are critical to their flourishing.

The enthusiasm of that group of ministers (I see you, IYM PTS Cohort I) and subsequent requests for more conversation about holy friendship confirmed what I was sensing: we need to prioritize our holy friendships because they are key contributors to our health and sustainability in ministry. Moreover, pastors and leaders who know the love of holy friends need to talk about them, model them, and cultivate the conditions for them to flourish in their communities.

I am confident pastors and leaders are healthier, more creative, and joyful and that they serve more effectively when they are supported by holy friends. These friends are a necessity, not a luxury. We remind one another of who we are called to be as children of God. We are cheer-leaders, confidants, and critics for one another. We recognize small wins as we seek to reach larger goals. When we feel lost, we reconnect one another to God's bigger story and remind one another that who we are and what we do matters and contributes to God's work in the world. We forgive one another when we cannot forgive ourselves. We defend one another fiercely when someone attacks us or, worse, we attack ourselves. We sustain and push one another to be the people God is shaping us to be. We help one another "look at God."

My hope and prayer is that you know the love of a holy friend, that you give love to a holy friend, and that you model holy friendship to others so the light and love of God shine through each of you and you all flourish in beloved community. Amen.

Notes

Preface

1   *Webster's New World College Dictionary* (New York: Houghton Mifflin Harcourt, 2014), s.v. "holy."

Chapter 1

1   Robin Dunbar, *Friends: Understanding the Power of Our Most Important Relationships* (London: Little, Brown, 2021), 3.

Chapter 2

1   Dunbar, *Friends*, 70–71.
2   Dunbar, 71.
3   Dunbar, 76.

Chapter 3

1   David Whyte, "Start Close In," in *River Flow: New & Selected Poems*, rev. ed. (Langley, WA: Many Rivers, 2015), 360–61.

Chapter 10

1   Daniel Victor, "He's 22. She's 81. Their Friendship Is Melting Hearts," *New York Times*, December 6, 2017, https://www.nytimes.com/2017/12/06/us/words-with -friends-meeting.html.

2   The story ran in more than fifty news outlets, including the *Washington Post, USA Today*, ABC, CBS, *People*, NPR, Huffington Post, the *Telegraph, Good Morning America, Inside Edition*, and BBC. It was the sixth most emailed piece from the *New York Times* the day it ran, December 6, 2017.

Exploring Further

This list highlights some resources that I have found particularly useful or comprehensive and suggests others that might extend your conversation on the chapter topics.

Barden, Mark, and Adam Morgan. *A Beautiful Constraint: How to Transform Your Limitations into Advantages, and Why It's Everyone's Business.* Hoboken, NJ: Wiley, 2015.

This is by far one of the most used resources in my work. Barden and Morgan describe how to view what we typically think of as challenges—such as lack of time, resources, and people (do these sound like the barriers to holy friendship?)—as opportunities for transforming people, institutions, and communities.

Brooks, Jonathan. *Church Forsaken: Practicing Presence in Neglected Neighborhoods.* Downers Grove, IL: IVP, 2018.

Brooks introduced me to the theology of place through this book. He challenges his readers to see loving their neighbors as loving their neighborhoods. *Church Forsaken* reminds us, regardless of where we live, to look for the image of God in all our neighbors, as in them, we just might find holy friends.

Dunbar, Robin. *Friends: Understanding the Power of Our Most Important Relationships*. London: Little, Brown, 2021.

Creator of Dunbar's number—that our capacity for friendship is limited to about 150 people—the author examines how and why friendships have a bigger influence on our happiness, health, and lifespan than anything else except quitting smoking. His use of social circles contributes to the framework for chapter 2 of this book.

Dunkelman, Marc J. *The Vanishing Neighbor: The Transformation of American Community*. New York: W. W. Norton, 2014.

Dunkelman's work alarmed me from the moment I picked up his book because he helped me make sense of a childhood experience. I would visit my father's hometown of Batesville, Arkansas, where his parents had lived in the same home for more than seventy years. My father's family knew literally everyone in town. My grandfather knew who to call to fix a chair, find a book, remember the date of an event, and learn when the next shipment of new cars was being delivered to the car lot. Batesville was like a foreign land to me and my city upbringing. Dunkelman identifies a shift in the structure of American life—the decline of our local communities and what he calls "middle-ring" relationships. His work with mapping the rings of society contributes to the foundation of chapter 2.

Faith & Leadership. https://faithandleadership.com/.

This website is a comprehensive learning resource for Christian leaders and their institutions from Leadership Education at Duke Divinity. You can easily search for

articles, essays, and interviews on holy friendship, thriving communities, vocation, Christian leadership, vibrant
institutions, and many other topics relevant to pastors
and leaders. Much of my original thinking about holy
friendship, especially using Greg Jones's definition before
I developed my own, can be found here.

Friedman, Ann, and Aminatou Sow. *Big Friendship: How
We Keep Each Other Close.* New York: Simon & Schuster,
2021.

Hosts of the hit podcast "Call Your Girlfriend," *New York
Times* best-selling authors Friedman and Sow record the
stories of their first decade of friendship and invite readers to consider how we form and preserve our friendships.

Gladwell, Malcolm. *Blink: The Power of Thinking without
Thinking.* New York: Little, Brown, 2005.

While everything Gladwell writes is genius, I am particularly
grateful for his articulation of a "blink" moment—when
you recognize something or someone "in the blink of an
eye." While much of this book is about carefully consider-
ing and challenging our thoughts formed in a blink, several
of the leaders I interviewed referred to knowing they had
found a friend, a kindred spirit, "in a blink" and attributed
their vocabulary to Gladwell.

Grant, Adam. *Give and Take: Why Helping Others Drives
Our Success.* London: Penguin, 2014.

Everything Grant writes is worthwhile. In *Give and Take*,
he explains why success is dependent on how we work
with and are in relationship with others. While he doesn't
use the language of holy friendship, similar frameworks of

trust, honesty, vulnerability, and accountability are key to his argument.

Hays, Katie. *We Were Spiritual Refugees: A Story to Help You Believe in Church*. Grand Rapids, MI: Eerdmans, 2020.

If you want to know how to create beloved community with those who are innately skeptical of all things church, Jesus, and organized religion, look no further. I read this as a love story between a church planter and the spiritual refugees who came together to build a church marked by radical welcome, deep curiosity, and unconditional love. Hays knows how to cultivate the conditions for holy friendships to flourish. In *We Were Spiritual Refugees*, she gifts us stories of her experiments, failures, and successes in a witty, whimsical, and wise way.

Jones, Gregory L. *Christian Social Innovation: Renewing Wesleyan Witness*. Nashville: Abingdon, 2016.

In this primer for Christian social innovation, Jones talks about how holy friends push one another to dream God-sized dreams for beloved community.

Mather, Michael. *Having Nothing, Possessing Everything: Finding Abundant Communities in Unexpected Places*. Grand Rapids, MI: Eerdmans, 2018.

Mather's book is his beautiful recollection of how relationships with his neighbors changed the way the church served the community. Holy friendships can be found throughout his stories because it is through friendship that the church truly became a neighborhood church.

Parker, Priya. *The Art of Gathering: How We Meet and Why It Matters*. New York: Riverhead, 2018.

Parker argues for a human-centered approach to gathering people that will create meaningful and memorable experiences. Churches and Christian institutions would greatly benefit by implementing even her most basic of strategies.

Pohl, Christine. *Living into Community: Cultivating Practices That Sustain Us*. Grand Rapids, MI: Eerdmans, 2011.

Pohl's work is a foundational text for helping churches and individuals build and sustain vibrant communities through practicing gratitude, promise-keeping, truth-telling, and hospitality.

Root, Andrew. *Pastor in a Secular Age: Ministry to People Who No Longer Need a God*. Ada, MI: Baker Academic, 2019.

Root explores how this secular age has impacted the identity and practice of the pastor, obscuring our core vocation: to call and assist others in the experience of ministry.

Whyte, David. *River Flow: New & Selected Poems*, rev. ed. Langley, WA: Many Rivers, 2015.

This collection of some of Whyte's earliest poems offers wisdom and beauty and reads like journal entries from our souls.